Kitchen Hints

Hilary Davies was born in Birmingham in 1949 and educated at school there and at Newnham College, Cambridge. She now lives in London where she works as a publisher's editor.

Like her first book, *Household Hints* (also available in Fontana), she has compiled *Kitchen Hints* because it's just what she needs: she hates cleaning, is prone to accidents, has a terrible memory, enjoys cooking well because she loves eating, but is always short of time and money, and suffers a complete blank whenever she's asked, 'What shall we have for dinner?'

Hilary Davies

Kitchen Hints

Fontana Paperbacks

First published by Fontana Paperbacks in 1982

Copyright © Hilary Davies 1982

Illustrations by Margaret Chamberlain
Set in 10 on 11 pt Times
Made and printed by William Collins Sons & Co. Ltd,
Glasgow

The hints and recipes in this book have been carefully
tested and presented, but as they are intended only as
suggestions, the author and publisher cannot be held
responsible for failure or resulting damage.

For my sister

Acknowledgements

I should like to thank everyone who has helped me to assemble *Kitchen Hints*, particularly my mother, Mrs Ann Davies, and my sister, Susan Lloyd, for their untiring hint-hunting; also Sonia Allison, Mrs H. Anderson, Mrs M. Cain, Mrs Jill Campbell, Susan Campbell, Margaret Chamberlain, Miss Anne Coates, Mrs S. Coyle, Mary Darroch, Mrs E. Dick, Mrs Hazel Dutton, Rose Elliot, Theodora FitzGibbon, Helen Fraser, Miss H. Gibbs, Jane Grigson, Mrs N. Hawkins, Nora Hyett, Mrs Lynn Jacob, Mrs Barbara Jeavons, Simon King, Prue Leith, Nora Lewis, Mrs Betty McKenzie, Mrs D. McMaster, Lucinda McNeile, Helen Martin, Nick Meanwell, Antoinette Parkes, Mrs D. Pike, Maureen Price, Delia Smith, Michael Smith, Katie Stewart, Marika Hanbury Tenison, Joyce Turnbull, Mrs C. Waldron, Mrs D. Wheelock, Mrs A. Whitehall, Mrs C. Whittle and Mrs Alma Wood.

Contents

Introduction   9

The Kitchen Garden   11
Storage   21
Thrift   30
Cleaning   37
Emergencies   49
Snacks and Starters   55
Simple Soups   63
Fish, Poultry and Meat   69
Storecupboard Standbys   79
Potatoes   87
Other Vegetables, and Salads   95
Bread and Cereals   102
Sauces and Seasonings   109
Ten-minute Puddings   117
Better Baking   124
Fruit and Preserves   133
Famous Hints   145

Weights and Measures   151
Index   153

Introduction

Kitchen Hints is a mixture of ancient and modern wisdom, bringing together traditional recipes, wartime economy measures, tips passed down through generations of housekeepers – with ingenious new solutions to the problems that arise even in today's kitchen equipped with freezers, cling-film and all mod cons.

The kitchen is the engine-room of the household, the centre for many different housekeeping activities: and so the hints that follow range over cleaning and laundry, as well as everything you can do to food – growing it or buying it, storing and preserving it, preparing and cooking it. You will find, for example, tips on cleaning silver and pine tables, washing silks and woollens, growing herbs and houseplants, choosing a butcher, keeping cheese longer or ripening pears, making quick pickled gherkins or jam that's guaranteed to set, chopping onions and peeling apples faster – and what to do with the peel. As well as general hints on cookery, such as how to make gravy without browning, or how to cook meat without losing the juices, there are also separate chapters on simple soups made in seconds, meals made out of potatoes – or things you can find in the cupboard – quick (but nutritious) snacks, and ten-minute puddings.

The kitchen is a place where many things can go wrong – from burnt stews to burnt fingers; and so there is a chapter on emergencies. It is also a place where much can be wasted – not only food and fuel, but time; and so there is a chapter on thrift. Finally, there is a collection of famous hints in which several well-known cookery writers pass on their favourite bits of kitchen wisdom.

The hints and recipes throughout the book are all designed to make kitchen work simpler and speedier, more economical and more fun. Whether you are a bedsit egg-boiler, a cordon-bleu entertainer or a family caterer, you surely suffer occasionally from lack of time, or money, or inspiration. I hope that *Kitchen Hints* will offer you all some cheering ideas.

The Kitchen Garden

Whether you have an acre, an allotment or just a windowsill, you'll find some hints in this chapter which will help to bring new fragrance and flavour to your kitchen garden. On the windowsill – indoors or out – you may have to confine yourself to herbs. If you haven't got green fingers – or the patience to wait for seeds to germinate – invest in young plants in spring. Repot them in good compost, give them sunshine and water, and you'll be able to keep yourself supplied with fresh parsley, basil, mint, sage, thyme, marjoram and almost any other herb you fancy. Of course some of these herbs make pretty houseplants, and you'll find here hints about caring for all sorts of plants in the house.

For those who have real walk-out gardens, there are ingenious suggestions about cuttings, seedlings, pests and compost; about which plants to grow close together and which to keep apart. You may want to try growing some of the more unusual culinary plants recommended here – such as dandelions, marigolds, nettles and nasturtiums. If your garden is tiny, or a patio, you may even want to try growing fruit trees in tubs. Whether it's a pot of basil or a prize-winning marrow, you know it will taste twice as good if you've grown it yourself.

Basil

Basil needs warmth, but will survive happily in Britain in a pot on the kitchen windowsill. Choose sweet basil (*Ocimum basilicum*) which has large leaves – about an inch (3 cm) long – rather than bush basil (*Ocimum minimum*), which has leaves so tiny that it seems a shame to pick them. Keep nipping off the top shoots to encourage a bushy growth, and remove the white flowers when they appear, and you will be able to continue harvesting leaves right through the autumn.

If growing basil out of doors, do not plant the seeds until May when there is no further danger of frost.

Borage

Borage is a very easy herb to grow. Sow seeds in March, out of doors or in a window box. They will germinate quickly and once mature the plants will re-seed themselves. Use in salads, and to make herbal tea. Pour a pint (500 ml) of boiling water on to an ounce (30 g) of borage, cover and leave for six minutes, then strain.

Cacti

Add crushed egg shells to the soil in which cacti are planted to give them extra calcium.

Chives

Chives take a lot of nutrients out of the soil and need fertilizing to encourage the growth of their green tops. They will grow happily indoors in pots.

Coffee against pests

A little unused ground coffee mixed with carrot seeds when they are planted will help to confuse and deter carrot fly.

Sprinkle used coffee grounds in the seed drill a week before planting beans or tomatoes, to counteract root rot.

Cold houseplants

On winter nights or during cold spells plants should be moved from windowsills to warmer parts of the house, because when they get very cold their roots cannot absorb moisture and they may suffer from drought.

Compost heap

Site your compost heap on soil and, if possible, under an overhanging tree, which will keep it sheltered but out of direct sunshine. Build up six-inch (15-cm) layers, starting with a layer of soil mixed with leaves and twigs, then straw, sawdust or garden refuse, then manure, bonemeal or wood ash, then more leaves, then kitchen waste such as eggshells, tealeaves, fish bones and vegetable peelings. When the pile is five feet (1·75 metres) high make airholes in it and cover with black plastic sheeting. Moisten it regularly; turn and mix after three weeks and then again three weeks later. Three months after that, the compost will be nearly black and sweet-smelling and ready to use.

Coriander

In the spring, crush some coriander seeds and plant in well drained soil. In about two weeks they will have germinated, and the leaves (which look like parsley) can be used in curries and with fish.

Dandelion

If you want to cultivate dandelions to make salads, blanch the leaves to make them less bitter by covering with upturned buckets, or lift them before the winter frosts and grow in pots indoors.

Dill

Do not plant dill near fennel as they are closely related and there is a danger of cross-pollination.

Feeding houseplants

Feed houseplants with melted snow, which is rich in minerals.
   Or, use the water in which eggs have been boiled.
   Or, use flat soda water.
   Or, use the water in which fish has been frozen.

Ferns

Feed ferns with leftover weak tea, or bury a used teabag in the soil beside the roots.
   Or, give them a teaspoon of castor oil or olive oil every three months.

Ferns and other houseplants which like humid conditions will flourish close to the laundry sink or washing machine.

Flower holders

Tie plastic hair-rollers together in a bunch to support cut flowers.

Or, use a raw potato inside a vase, making holes in it first with a knitting needle.

If the stems of cut flowers are very short and difficult to arrange, stick them into wax drinking straws.

Fruit trees in tubs

If you are short of space in your kitchen garden you can grow apple, pear and other fruit trees in tubs. Suitable varieties of apple are Discovery and Laxton's Superb, and of pear, Conference and Williams' Bon Chrétien. Plant them in February or March if they have been growing in open ground, but at any time of year if they have been reared in containers. Use containers at least one foot (30 cm) across, line the bottom with broken flowerpots or pebbles for drainage, then pack firmly with potting compost. Leave two inches (5 cm) headroom for watering, and water the trees generously – every day in summer. Feed with a liquid fertilizer from April to September.

Keep in a sheltered place during the winter. When the blossom starts to appear in spring, you may want to protect it from birds by covering the tree with an old net curtain. Prune lightly back to the strongest buds in summer.

Repot in fresh compost every second spring.

Sowing herb seeds

Sow herb seeds in March or April in shallow drills. Mix the seeds with a little sharp sand which retains moisture and also deters slugs. When the seeds have germinated water frequently, then thin out when the plants are about two inches (5 cm) high.

Horseradish

To propagate horseradish, plant slivers of root in trenches two feet (60 cm) deep with plenty of manure or compost. Dig up in October or November when the roots are about ten inches (25 cm) long, and store in a cool damp place.

Leaking vase

A leak in a vase can be repaired with a few drops of melted candle wax.

Lovage

Because lovage is such a tall, sturdy plant it is useful for protecting other herbs from wind and cold weather. Use in salads and soups.

Marigolds

Grow marigolds to use the petals in place of saffron, to add colour and flavour to rice and other dishes. Steep the petals for a few minutes in hot stock before using.

Garlic spray

To eradicate wireworms, slugs, caterpillars and weevils, chop 3 oz (75 g) of garlic and mix with two teaspoons of mineral oil. Leave for twenty-four hours, then add a pint (575 ml) of water in which two teaspoons of soft soap have been dissolved. Stir thoroughly and strain into a plastic container to store. To use, dissolve one part of this mixture with twenty parts of water, and spray on to the leaves of affected vegetables and the soil around them.

To preserve heather

Wash a large raw potato and make holes in one side of it with a knitting needle. Insert the stems of heather in these to make a pretty arrangement which will stay fresh for months.

Milk spray

Spray milk on to apples and lettuces to control mildew. For large areas, dilute one part milk in nine parts water.

Or, dissolve 1 lb (450 g) of dried milk in a little hot water and then add to 1 gallon (4 litres) of cold water. Spray on to tomatoes, lettuces and cucumbers when planting, and then every ten days.

Mint

To stop mint spreading, surround the plant with pieces of slate pushed vertically into the ground.

Nasturtiums

Plant nasturtiums in your herb garden or window box: they are rich in vitamin C and are said to keep neighbouring plants healthy. Grow them alongside brassicas, peas and beans, and aphids will be attracted to them rather than to the vegetables.

Nasturtiums are good for people too: their flowers and leaves, when young and fresh, can be eaten in salads (remove the stalks which have a bitter taste). And their seeds can be pickled and used instead of capers. (Harvest when large and green, soak in salted water for twenty-four hours, then drain, put into a jar and cover with boiling spiced vinegar. Seal at once: they improve with keeping.)

Nettles

Nettles stimulate the growth of other plants, improve the quality of root vegetables and tomatoes and strengthen their resistance in disease. They can be used to make soups – and an excellent garden fertilizer.

Parsley

To grow parsley indoors, fill pots three-quarters full with potting compost, pour over it some water that has boiled and cooled, sprinkle a few parsley seeds on top and cover with a fine layer of dry compost. Stand on a saucer and keep moist with warm water. It may take up to six weeks for the seeds to germinate, but once the parsley is growing it will re-seed itself and provide a continuous supply for cooking.

If you are growing parsley out of doors you will need to plant new seeds each spring.

Keep cutting off parsley flower stalks to prevent the plant from flowering and going to seed. Harvest the leaves frequently to encourage new growth.

Pests

Grow strong-smelling herbs among your vegetables to deter pests. For example, rosemary will protect beans against weevils; rosemary, sage, thyme or mint will keep cabbage moths away from brassicas; basil keeps flies away from potatoes; chives deter aphids; mint deters ants; garlic protects potatoes against blight and horseradish protects them against beetles.

Some vegetables help to keep pests off others: for example, rhubarb protects beans against blackfly; leeks protect carrots against carrot flies; celery keeps moths away from cabbage; tomatoes keep beetles away from asparagus; lettuce protects radishes; and onions protect beetroot.

Flowers can also protect vegetables in this way. Zinnias keep most pests away from cucumbers, melons and marrows; marigolds protect beans; and a tall relative of the marigold called *Tagetes minuta* keeps pests away from beans, potatoes, tomatoes and strawberries.

Plant enemies

Never plant peas close to garlic, or onions near to strawberries.

Pre-heated soil

Warm up and dry out the ground where seeds are to be sown by putting cloches in place two weeks beforehand. The seeds will then germinate more quickly.

Home-made propagator

Cut the bottom off a large, plastic, soft drinks bottle and invert it over a flowerpot to make a perfect individual propagator. (A 3-pint [1½-litre] bottle fits a four-inch [10-cm] pot; a 4-pint [2-litre] bottle fits a five-inch [12·5-cm] pot.) Don't throw the top of the bottle away: it can be used as another propagator, or as a funnel.

Rose cuttings

Make a hole in a raw potato with a knitting needle, insert a rose cutting in it and plant in the garden. The potato will keep the plant moist while it forms roots.

Seedlings

Use a baby's feeding cup to water young seedlings with a very gentle spray.

Sweet potato plant

To grow your own unusual and inexpensive houseplant, put a sweet potato in a glass jar with water, leaving about one-third of the potato uncovered. Stand it in a warm light place and it will soon develop roots and – after about two weeks – pretty red shoots with green leaves. Keep adding water, as the plant may drink up to two pints (1 litre) a day.

Window boxes

Sprinkle gravel on top of your kitchen window boxes to prevent rain splashing mud on to the window.

Wooden stakes

Use chestnut or elm sticks to make stakes for supporting vegetables. Peel them and dip in a preservative before putting in position.

Young plants

Cut off the top and bottom of an empty plastic bottle and place it in the ground around a tender young plant to protect it. When the plant is firmly established, simply cut the bottle away.

Give extra protection during frosty weather to tender young plants in an unheated greenhouse by covering them at night with several layers of newspaper.

Storage

It's no use being a brilliant bargain-spotter or a patient menu-planner if you don't also take care over storage. What could be more frustrating than to find at the last minute that the vital ingredient in your special bargain-treat meal has gone off?

You may say you need a freezer; or, if you're a romantic like me, you may daydream of a cool, dry, airy, walk-in larder with a gauze-covered window. But in reality most of us are stuck with a fridge. The hints that follow show how, nevertheless, you can keep fruit and vegetables, salads and herbs, meat, fish and dairy products in perfect condition until you need them. And don't forget that your fridge needs looking after as well. Defrost it frequently, keep it clean and fresh, wrap up foods that smell strongly, and don't put cooked foods into it until they are completely cold.

There are hints here about tinned and frozen foods, too. The crucial thing is to keep tabs on them: if you're super-efficient you'll write on tinned and dry goods the date when you bought them, so that they're used in rotation and not stored for too long. If you have a freezer you'll follow instructions about blanching and open-freezing and thawing times; you'll label and date everything; and you may even keep a freezer-register to show you at a glance what you have in stock.

But remember that whatever you are storing or freezing must be absolutely fresh to start with. Learn to recognize the signs of freshness and good quality in fruit and vegetables and meat and fish. Always check sell-by dates. And if you find something is *not* perfect when you get it home, then take it back and complain. You're paying for freshness, so make sure you get your money's worth.

Avocados

If your avocados are ripe but you don't want to eat them yet, store them in the refrigerator to stop them ripening further.

Bananas

If you put bananas in the fridge their skins will darken, but the flesh will stay firm.

Basil

To preserve the delicious flavour of fresh basil leaves, store them in oil with a little salt added. When you have used up all the basil, you can use the oil to make a basil-flavoured salad dressing.

Brie

If you find your Brie is chalky, scrape the outside with a fork to allow the cheese to breathe. The skin may turn brown, but the cheese will be much more succulent.

Cakes

Tins are better than plastic boxes for storing cakes, because plastic is porous and may not give an airtight seal, and also because it tends to harbour smells.

Don't store fruit cakes in silver foil for a long time, or the acid in the fruit may corrode the foil and form a mould.

Cheese

Pretty china cheese dishes simply don't keep cheese fresh. Wrap it in greaseproof paper and a polythene bag and store at the bottom of the refrigerator, but bring it out at least an hour before eating so that it is served at room temperature.

If you smear the cut edge of a piece of hard cheese thinly with butter each time it is wrapped and put back in the fridge, it will stay fresher longer.

Cold cheese is harder and therefore easier to grate. If you have to do a lot of cheese grating put the cheese in the freezing compartment of the fridge for a quarter of an hour first. •

Cream

Store cartons of double or sour cream upside down in the refrigerator and they will keep fresh longer.

Damp cupboard

If your larder is damp, place a bowl of lime on a shelf to dry the air.

Freezing fish

Empty, wax, fruit juice cartons can be used for freezing fish in. Rinse thoroughly, add the fish, fill up with water and staple shut.

Freezing fruit

Acid fruits and vegetables, such as apples, rhubarb and tomatoes, should be wrapped in polythene for freezing and not foil, as the acid in them might react with the foil and split it.

Ripening fruit

If your pears, peaches or tomatoes are under-ripe, put them in a brown paper bag with a ripe apple. Make a few holes in the bag and then leave overnight in a cool, dark place.

Game

Sprinkle game with freshly ground coffee to keep it sweet for several days. Do the same if you are packing game to transport it.

Lettuce

A lettuce will stay fresh for several days if stored in a tightly lidded saucepan, or wrapped in newspaper in a cool place.

Meat

Unwrap fresh meat as soon as you get it home from the butcher, and store it loosely covered with paper in the fridge. Take it out of the fridge an hour before cooking, otherwise it will take longer to cook than the recipe says.

Cooked meat

Allow joints of meat to get completely cold, then wrap loosely in foil, cling-film or greaseproof paper to prevent the meat from drying out. Store in the refrigerator for up to two days; do not slice or mince it until you need it.

Melons

Store in plastic bags in the refrigerator so that they do not absorb smells from other food. Some people like to serve melons chilled, straight from the fridge; but if you bring them out an hour before serving so that they reach room temperature you will find that they have more flavour.

Mozzarella

Keep in its plastic bag and store in a bowl of cold water in the fridge.

Mushrooms

Store mushrooms in a cool dark place – and not in the fridge.

Olives

If you buy olives in brine wash them off and store them in a jar of oil. They will stay fresh like this and, when you have finished the olives, you will be left with delicious olive-flavoured oil for making salad dressings.

Parsley

Wash fresh parsley, shake dry and store in a plastic bag in the freezer compartment. When it is thoroughly frozen you can simply crumble off what you need, without having to chop it.

(See also Jane Grigson's hint, page 148.)

Identifying pies

When making pies which will be stored in the freezer, prick the tops in the shape of the first letter of their contents – C for chicken, A for apple, etc. – to save labelling.

Plastic bags

Use clip-type wooden or plastic clothes pegs to reseal polythene bags containing food. It's quicker and simpler than using wire twists.

Refrigerator smells

To get rid of unpleasant smells, put a saucerful of charcoal in your refrigerator.

Freezing sausages

When open-freezing sausages, line the tray with a sheet of polythene to stop the sausages sticking.

Freezing soups

Line plastic boxes with polythene bags to freeze soups. When the soup has frozen solid the bag can be lifted out and put directly in the freezer.

Save two-pint (1-litre) milk or fruit juice cartons for freezing stock or soup. Line the carton with a plastic bag, open-freeze, and when frozen wrap in a second bag before returning to the freezer.

Stock cubes

Store stock cubes in the fridge and they will be easier to crumble.

Tinned asparagus

Open tins of asparagus at the bottom, otherwise you risk damaging the tips when you get them out.

Tinned foods

If you use only part of a tin of food – especially something acidic, like tomatoes or apple purée – do not leave the remainder in the tin or it may deteriorate.

Tinned meat

If you put a tin of ham or corned beef in the fridge for a few minutes before opening it you will find it easier to slice.

Watercress

Keep watercress fresh by storing it in a bowl of cold water, with the stems uppermost.

An approximate guide to recommended maximum
fridge and freezer storage

	Fridge days	Freezer months
Dairy		
Butter (salted)	14	3
(unsalted)	14	6
Cheese (hard)	10	–
(soft)	5	6
Cream	3	3
Eggs (fresh)	14	–
(hard-boiled)	7	–
Egg whites	4	9
Egg yolks	3	9
Lard and margarine	21	5
Milk (homogenized)	4	1
Meat		
Bacon (smoked rashers, joints)	7	2
(unsmoked rashers, joints)	7	1
Beef joints	3	12
Chops and steaks	3	6
Lamb, pork and veal joints	3	6
Mince and offal	1	3
Sausages	1	6
Stews, casseroles, etc.	2	3

	Fridge days	*Freezer* months
Poultry and game		
Chicken (fresh)	2	12
(cooked: remove stuffing)	2	2
Duck	2	4
Game birds	2	7
Goose	2	4
Turkey	2	6
Venison	2	12
Fish		
Cooked fish	2	2
Oily fish	1	2
Shellfish	1	1
Smoked fish	2	3
White fish	1	3

Thrift

Thrift has a reputation for being dull, but here are some thrifty ideas that rely on ingenuity and imagination. If you are able to improvise or make your own substitutes when you've run out; to make something out of nothing – or at least out of leftovers – when you're broke; and to experiment with unfamiliar ingredients when they are plentiful and cheap – then your cooking is going to be a lot more interesting as well as economical.

It's common sense not to waste fuel in the kitchen. Whenever possible, cook two things at once: steam one vegetable on top of another, or bake and roast things simultaneously in the oven. And don't waste hot water. Wash all the dishes at once, instead of bits and pieces as you go along.

But my favourite thrifty kitchen hint is: don't waste time. The stew won't taste any better if you hang around sniffing it while it cooks. (If you keep peeping at it it will actually taste worse, because you'll let flavour escape.) Don't keep prodding and stirring things to see if they're done. Do some time and motion studies on your kitchen activities. If you have to wait for something precarious to come to the boil, use the time to chop something else, or clean something – or read the paper. Get organized so that time-saving becomes a habit. For example, when you first go into the kitchen to start preparing a meal, remember to: (1) set the oven at the temperature you need; (2) arrange the oven shelves as you want them; and (3) put plates and serving dishes to warm.

So, sort out your priorities. It may be admirable in some ways to turn that bit of leftover chicken into a masterpiece; but is it going to take hours of your precious time? No one else is going to enjoy the meal either if you sit down exhausted and grim after slaving resentfully over it all day. Remember: think of the cook as well as the cooking.

Baby foods

Heat an individual portion of baby food gently and economically in an egg poacher.

Leftover beer

Add a little sugar to leftover beer to stop it going flat, and store in an airtight jar to use for cooking.

Butter

It is wasteful to use unsalted butter in cooking as a base for savoury sauces, when the flavour is disguised. Use a cheaper salted brand instead. Use unsalted butter only for cooking sweet things, such as sweet omelettes. And for pastry and cakes, use margarine or a mixture of half lard and half margarine.

If you are making a lot of sandwiches, beat a little warm milk into your butter to soften it and make it go further.

If a new packet of butter is inclined to stick to the wrapper, run it under the cold tap for a minute and the paper will peel off easily.

Home-made buttermilk

Add two pints (1 litre) of made-up powdered milk to a small carton of commercial buttermilk. Add a pinch of salt, cover, leave overnight, then chill. Store in the fridge, and as you use the buttermilk keep topping it up with powdered milk.

Chocolate

Buy half-price chocolate Father Christmases and Easter bunnies in post-holiday sales and use the chocolate for cooking.

Cream substitute

Use natural yoghurt as a cheaper substitute for cream and sour cream in cooking. Stabilize it first if you wish to stop it separating out (page 54).

Home-made curd cheese

Line a nylon sieve with muslin or first-aid gauze, place over a bowl and pour into it fresh natural yoghurt. Leave for six hours, until you have whey in the bowl and curds in the sieve. Use like cottage cheese, adding herbs and seasonings to it if you wish.

Saving fuel

Save fuel by steaming a second vegetable over the pan in which potatoes or rice are boiling. Place them in a colander if you haven't got a steaming basket, and cover with the saucepan lid.

In the same way, steam fillets of fish on an ovenproof plate over boiling potatoes.

Heat plates quickly, and save fuel, by putting them for a few minutes in place of lids on saucepans cooking on the stove.

Kidneys in sherry sauce

For 4 people: core and halve 8 lamb's kidneys and fry gently in 1 oz (25 g) of butter for 3 minutes. Remove from pan and add another 1 oz (25 g) butter with a chopped onion. Cook gently for 5 minutes, then return the kidneys to the pan and blend in 1 tablespoon of flour. Cook for 1 minute, then stir in ½ pint (275 ml) of chicken stock, and simmer for 5 minutes. Add salt, freshly ground black pepper and 2 tablespoons of sherry, then serve sprinkled with chopped parsley, on a bed of rice.

Leftovers

To reheat a meal of leftovers for one or two people thriftily, put them in separate jam jars and stand in simmering water in a large pan.

Meatballs

For 4 people: mix together 1 lb (450 g) minced cooked meat, 1 grated onion, 1 beaten egg, 3 crustless slices of bread soaked in milk, some salt, pepper, a pinch of nutmeg and a little chopped parsley. With floured hands roll into twenty small balls and fry in hot fat or oil until evenly browned.

Serve with fresh tomato sauce (page 116) or Greek lemon sauce (page 110) and rice or pasta.

Mince

Add a handful of oatmeal or grated raw potato to 1 lb (450 g) of mince to make an extra portion.

Oxtail stew

For 4 people: wipe and trim fat from 1 jointed oxtail, then sear in 2 oz (50 g) dripping and remove from pan. Soften 2 chopped rashers of streaky bacon, 2 chopped carrots, 2 chopped onions and 2 chopped sticks of celery in the pan for 5 minutes, then blend in 2 tablespoons of flour and cook for 2 minutes, stirring. Return oxtail to pan with 2 pints (1 litre) of beef stock, 2 bay leaves, a handful of parsley, 6 black peppercorns and salt, cover and simmer gently for 4 hours, skimming fat from surface occasionally. Add the juice of half a lemon, and sprinkle with chopped fresh parsley. Serve with hot crusty bread and a green salad.

Pet food dishes

Save polystyrene trays from supermarket meat to use as disposable pet food dishes.

Picnic bottles

Save empty pill bottles and use them to take salad dressing or sauces on picnics.

Pie plates

It is more economical to buy cheap ovenproof plates for baking, freezing and reheating pies than to buy foil plates which have a shorter life.

Rissoles

For 2 people: combine 8 oz (225 g) finely minced cooked meat with 1 small finely chopped onion, 1 beaten egg, 2 heaped tablespoons of fresh breadcrumbs, some salt, pepper, 2 tablespoons of chopped fresh parsley and, if you wish, a crushed clove of garlic and a pinch of cinnamon. Mix well, form into cake shapes, coat in seasoned flour and fry for 5 minutes on each side in hot oil.

Salad soup

Don't throw away leftover salad, even if it's dressed. Put it in a liquidizer with a tin of tomato juice, a dash of Worcester sauce and Tabasco, blend and season to taste. Serve chilled.

Stale sandwiches

Recycle stale sandwiches by dipping them in a mixture of 1 beaten egg with 3 tablespoons of milk and then frying in oil or butter until golden on both sides.

Home-made scoop

Plastic soft drinks bottles with handles can be cut up and used as scoops for flour or sugar – or sand in sand pits.

Scrambled eggs

Add a spoonful of white breadcrumbs to eggs before scrambling to improve the flavour and make the eggs go further.

Sour milk

Don't throw away sour milk or cream: it can be used in baking and will make your cakes or pancakes fluffier.

Fried sweetbreads

For 4 people: prepare 1 lb (450 g) of lamb's or calf's sweet-breads (see page 78). When cold, slice and dip into beaten egg and breadcrumbs and fry quickly in deep fat or oil. Serve with fried bacon, tartare sauce (page 116) and rice.

Weighing syrup

To weigh syrup, honey, molasses, etc., economically, rather than letting it stick to the scales, put the whole tin or jar on the scales first, then take out spoonfuls until the weight has gone down by however much you need.

Tomato ketchup

If you do not shake the bottle,
    First none will come and then a lot'll.

Leftover wine

Add small quantities of leftover wine to wine vinegar to extend it indefinitely.

Leftover wine intended for cooking can be frozen until required.

Cleaning

I don't believe that any number of hints can make cleaning fun. However I do think there is a certain satisfaction to be gained from learning how to solve classic cleaning problems less arduously. Everyone, for example, surely hates cleaning windows: but try using the ammonia and vinegar and cornflour polish on page 46, and you'll find the job almost magically easy. Especially if you finish off with good old-fashioned crumpled newspaper.... Or try the hints for cleaning burnt saucepans, or caramel saucepans, or scrambled egg saucepans: they're all ingenious, and simple, and sure.

If you're a keen cleaner of course you'll never let dirt build up or get ground in to carpets, because you know that makes it more difficult to remove. You'll clean little and often. You'll probably even have a rota, and clean one room a day. You'll certainly keep your brushes and dusters in good order, and empty your vacuum cleaner bag *before* it's jam-packed. You won't have much to learn from the chapter that follows.

But for the rest of us, these tips will make life a little brighter. In general, the good news is that you don't need all sorts of new-fangled polishes and sprays and creams for cleaning. Keep plenty of salt, white vinegar, lemon juice and bicarbonate of soda in the broom cupboard as well as in the pantry, and you'll find that these – along with household ammonia and bleach – are far more essential, and versatile, and economical, aids.

Aluminium saucepans

Clean with crumpled silver foil.

Or, add two teaspoons of cream of tartar to two pints (1 litre) of water in the stained pan and boil for ten minutes.

Don't leave cooked food in aluminium saucepans for a long time as the metal may react with acids in the food and sour it.

Barbecue grill

Rub with oil before use to prevent food sticking and make cleaning easier.

Clean with leftover real coffee.

Quick beeswax polish

Grate 3 oz (75 g) beeswax and 2 oz (50 g) paraffin wax into 1 pint (500 ml) of pure turpentine. Warm gently in a double boiler or a basin standing in a pan of simmering water, until the waxes dissolve. (Take great care because the turpentine is highly inflammable.) Meanwhile dissolve 1 tablespoon of pure soapflakes in 1 pint (500 ml) of hot water, and add this to the other ingredients. Continue heating until thoroughly blended and creamy, then cool and store in a screw-top jar.

NB You can buy beeswax in small blocks in hardware shops. Paraffin wax is usually available in chain chemists, but if you can't get it use white household candles instead.

Save old tobacco tins and use them to transfer small amounts of your home-made polish to as you use it.

Brass

To prevent brass tarnishing in damp weather, clean first with metal polish (or a cut lemon dipped in salt), then apply a little petroleum jelly with a soft cloth. Polish with a dry duster.

After cleaning brass, rub it with crumpled newspaper and then give it a final polish with a soft duster. This gives a bright, lasting shine, and leaves your dusters cleaner.

Brass handles

If you have to replace old brass handles with new ones and you don't like their lacquered shininess, clean them with metal polish. This will remove the lacquer so that they can get nicely tarnished.

Burnt saucepans

Leave to soak overnight filled with a solution of bleach in water.

Or, put a tablespoon of washing powder into the pan, fill up to the burn mark with warm or cold water, and leave to stand for an hour. Wash in warm soapy water, and the pan will be as good as new.

Caramel saucepans

To clean a saucepan after making caramel, fill it with warm water and bring it to the boil.

Cast-iron frying pans

Clean by heating the empty pan and rubbing in salt with a kitchen towel.

Or, heat a teaspoon of oil in the pan and then rub this in with a kitchen towel.

If the enamel lining of a cast-iron pan becomes discoloured soak it overnight in a solution of biological washing powder.

Ceramic tiles

Ceramic tiles can be cleaned and polished with crumpled newspaper.

Chicken bricks

Clean porous chicken or fish bricks by soaking them in hot water with two teaspoons of salt. Don't use washing-up liquid on them, as they might absorb a soapy flavour.

Chrome

Clean with dry bicarbonate of soda on a dry cloth.

Or, polish with surgical spirit.

Or, use ammonia in hot water.

Cleaning products

There's no need to have a host of cleaning products in your cupboard. Just keep one ammonia-based liquid cleaner to use neat on cookers, stubborn pans or wash-hand basins, etc., and diluted for everything else including kitchen floors.

Condensation

A cup of salt placed on a window ledge will absorb moisture from the air and keep your window free of condensation.

Cookers

A neat and dramatic way of cleaning all the fiddly bits of a cooker, if they have been badly neglected, is to put all the removable parts into a dustbin bag, take it out of doors, pour in two cups of household ammonia, fasten with a tie and leave outside for several hours. The fumes from the ammonia will loosen stubborn dirt, and afterwards you can rinse the whole lot clean with a garden hose.

Decanters

To clean a dull decanter, put into it a handful of cooking salt and two teaspoons of white vinegar. Shake vigorously, then rinse.

Or, put in a handful of crushed eggshells, a pint of water and a teaspoon of vinegar, shake and rinse.

If you want to dry a decanter quickly before putting wine into it, aim warm air from a hairdryer into it for a few minutes.

Or, warm it gently in a slow oven and then blow cold air into it – either with a hairdryer or with bellows.

Alternatively, if you want to dry a decanter or vase thoroughly in order to put it on display in your glass cabinet, rinse it out with about a tablespoon of methylated spirit. Tip out the excess, and all remaining traces of the spirit will evaporate. But remember to rinse with water before using for wine.

Impregnated dusters

Sprinkle flannelette dusters with paraffin, roll them up over-night and then hang outside to air for an hour. They will give a lovely sheen to wooden furniture – without any polish.

Floors

If your kitchen floor is dull after you have swept and mopped it, wipe over it again with a solution of white vinegar in warm water (a teacupful of vinegar to a bucket of water).

Floury basins

After making cakes or pastry, rinse floury basins first in cold water. Hot water hardens the flour and makes it more difficult to remove.

Glass

Never put precious glass in the dishwasher: the detergent in dishwasher powder may damage it, leaving filmy marks on the surface which are impossible to remove.

Add vinegar to washing-up rinsing water to make glasses shine.

Graters

If you hate cleaning graters, use a potato peeler instead to grate small amounts of chocolate or cheese.

Irons

To clean the bottom of an iron that is stained or sticky, first make sure that the iron is unplugged and cool, then rub the stain with a cloth that has been dipped in methylated spirit and vinegar. Never try to clean an iron with steel wool.

Kettles

Prevent fur forming in a kettle by keeping several glass marbles in it.

Or, wipe the inside regularly with a damp cloth.

Linoleum

Clean linoleum with a solution of half a teacup of bleach and a quarter of a cup each of white vinegar and washing soda in one gallon (4 litres) of warm water.

Remove heel marks from linoleum or vinyl by rubbing with paraffin or turpentine.

Non-stick pans

If you have a non-stick pan which has become blackened and tacky with carbonized particles of fat and oil, fill it up with a solution of two tablespoons of baking soda in one cup of household bleach and two cups of water. Use larger quantities if necessary to fill the pan. Bring to the boil and simmer for ten minutes, then rinse. (It smells dreadful but it works!)

Ovens

If food is spilled while cooking in the oven, sprinkle it with salt. Afterwards, when the oven is cool, it will be easier to wipe clean.

PVC chairs

Never use polish or detergents on PVC, but simply clean with soap and water, then rinse with clear water.

Refrigerators

To keep a refrigerator sweet and fresh, wipe after defrosting with a solution of one tablespoon of bicarbonate of soda in two pints (1 litre) of warm water.

Scrambled egg pans

Avoid saucepan cleaning by scrambling eggs in a buttered basin standing in a pan of simmering water.

Silver

To clean silver cutlery effectively and economically, save silver foil until you have a jam-jarful, then put it in a saucepan, cover with water and boil hard for fifteen minutes. Cool the liquid and store in a screw-top jar. Dip tarnished silver in it, then rinse and polish with a soft cloth.

Or, put a cupful of washing soda in a large bowl with two pints (1½ litres) of boiling water, stir until dissolved and add a few pieces of silver foil. Put silver cutlery in this and it will almost at once become beautifully clean. (Take care not to immerse handles in the liquid or they may become loosened.) Rinse and polish.

Sinks

To clean a badly stained sink, line it with paper towels and pour household bleach over them. Leave for half an hour, then remove the towels and it will be easy to wipe away the loosened grime.

Stainless steel

Remove rust marks by rubbing with cigarette lighter fuel.

Remove other stains with methylated spirit, white vinegar, or soda from a syphon.

Kitchen tables

To lift the dirt from an old wooden kitchen table, sprinkle tablespoons of oxalic acid (which you can buy at the chemist) into a bowl of boiling water and sponge this on to the table until it is thoroughly soaked. When dry, sponge again with clean hot water.

Tablecloths

If sauce or gravy is spilt during a meal and the cloth cannot instantly be put into cold water to soak, sprinkle talcum powder on the stain as an interim measure, to absorb the colour and grease.

Toothbrushes

Save old toothbrushes and keep them by the sink for fiddly jobs like cleaning graters, blenders, tap bottoms and toasters. Sterilize them first in boiling water.

Venetian blinds

Dip a cloth in surgical or methylated spirit, wrap it round a spatula and use to clean between the slats.

Walls

If grease is splashed on your kitchen wallpaper, dab on a little talcum powder or French chalk. Repeat if necessary as it absorbs the grease, then brush off after a few hours.

Windows

Use horizontal strokes to clean one side of the window and vertical strokes for the other: then you'll know which side the smears are on.

Avoid the problem of smears altogether by cleaning windows with a solution of six tablespoons each of household ammonia and white vinegar with two tablespoons of cornflour in a bucket of warm water. When nearly dry, polish with crumpled newspaper.

Wood

Paper that is stuck to wood can be removed by moistening with baby oil. After a few minutes it will peel away easily.

Pests

Cockroaches

To deter cockroaches, sprinkle washing soda in the cracks where they appear.

Dustbin raiders

To stop roaming animals attacking your dustbin, sprinkle the bags with a little household ammonia.

Flies

Hang bunches of lavender at your window to keep flies away.

Mice

To deter mice, paint round mouseholes with oil of peppermint, which they hate.

Laundry

Coca Cola

Leftover Coca Cola added to the wash will help to remove greasy stains.

Fabric softener

White vinegar is a cheap and effective fabric softener: just add two tablespoons to each wash. (It doesn't leave a smell.)

Feathers

When spin-drying feather pillows or down-filled quilts or anoraks, put a clean tennis shoe in, too, to balance the load.

Nylon

To whiten yellowing nylon, mix one gallon (4 litres) of hot water with six tablespoons of dishwasher detergent and three tablespoons of household bleach. Cool to room temperature, then soak the nylon garments in this for half an hour. Rinse in cool water with a dash of white vinegar (the vinegar neutralizes the bleach).

Overflows

If your washing machine overflows with lather because you have used soapflakes by mistake, squeeze a little lemon juice into the soap powder compartment. The bubbles will disappear at once.

Alternatively, sprinkle salt into the soap powder compartment.

Polyester

If a white polyester garment has gone off-white, soak it overnight in a gallon of water mixed with a cupful of dishwasher detergent. Next day wash as usual.

Silk

Add a couple of sugar lumps to the rinsing water when washing silk, to give the fabric more body.

Sock hanger

Peg socks and stockings in pairs on a coathanger, then take it out and peg the coathanger on the washing line. This saves you catching cold, saves space on the line, and saves time getting them in when it starts to rain.

Thrifty washing

If you don't have a huge quantity of washing, don't waste washing powder and electricity by running your machine half-full: wash white things one week and coloured things the next.

It saves electricity if you use cooler water in your washing machine. If you have a cold-fill machine, keep the heater at a lower temperature. If you do this you may need to prepare your own washing powder solution, because British soap powder manufacturers are not yet marketing a powder which dissolves in cold water. Make your own solution by dissolving your usual powder in a little boiling water, then cool and store to add to the wash as required.

Woollens

If you run out of liquid detergent you can wash woollens just as safely and effectively with shampoo.

Emergencies

An extraordinary number of crises can arise in the kitchen, mostly as a result of either shortage or excess. To avoid the first kind of problem you really need to be super-efficient, and not only *notice* what you're about to run out of, but also compose a shopping list to remind yourself to replace it. But in case you're not this well organized, here are some hints about managing without, or what to use instead.

Restraint is the rule for avoiding the second kind of emergency. If you're cooking something unfamiliar, for example (especially if it's in large quantities), use at first only half as much seasoning as the recipe says, then taste, and add more if necessary. Don't leave food cooking on a fierce heat, but on a gentle simmer. And if your sense of time is erratic, or you can't rely on your oven temperature, it's probably worth investing in some thermometers.

Of course it isn't only food that gets damaged in the kitchen. Cooks are exposed to all sorts of hazards, from burns and scalds to chapped hands, aching feet – and life-shortening panic. So do take care of yourself and remember that you're far more important than the cooking. Don't give yourself unnecessary anxieties by tackling complicated dishes when you're short of time, or have lots of guests. Don't be over-concerned if the food isn't scorching hot when it gets to the table (people would only have to blow on it). And apart from sitting down to string the beans, and that kind of thing, keep the following hints handy to help set your mind at rest.

Unidentified basins

Measure the volume of each of your cooking basins and dishes and mark it on the bottom in bright nail varnish – to save guessing when you need a certain size in a hurry.

Brown sugar

If you run out of brown sugar when baking, use white sugar and molasses instead. A tablespoon of molasses for every 8 oz (225 g) of sugar is equivalent to soft brown sugar; two tablespoons of molasses mixed with 8 oz (225 g) white sugar will taste like dark brown.

Burns

To soothe a burn, apply a paste of bicarbonate of soda and water.

Burnt stew

If a stew dries out and burns, do not stir it. Tip it into a clean saucepan, leaving behind the burnt bits on the bottom, add more liquid if necessary, and if it still tastes burnt add a little more seasoning – pepper or chilli powder or Worcester sauce.

Chapped hands

Rub equal parts of sugar and dripping into chapped hands: this is a simple and effective cure.

Chocolate

If you run out of plain chocolate when baking, use cocoa powder and melted butter instead (one teaspoon of butter will bind four tablespoons of cocoa).

Coffee filters

If you run out of coffee filters, use a paper kitchen towel to filter coffee instead.

Cook's feet

Rub a little methylated spirit into the soles of your feet to revive them after a hard day in the kitchen.

Cream

If you run out of single cream, melt 4 oz (125 g) of unsalted butter in ¼ pint (150 ml) of milk. Heat but do not boil. Then blend in a liquidizer for 10 seconds and leave to cool, stirring occasionally.

If you run out of whipping cream, heat 4 oz (125 g) of

unsalted butter with ½ pint (275 ml) of top-of-the-milk and ½ teaspoon of gelatine until the butter has melted. Do not boil. Liquidize, then chill until firm.

If you can't get sour cream when you need it for a recipe, use instead a mixture of half fresh cream (single or double) and half natural yoghurt.

Dried-up ham

If sliced ham has gone hard you can revive it by soaking it in milk for a few minutes.

Fatty soup

Use paper kitchen towels to soak up fat from the surface of soups or stews.

Fire

If a chip pan or grill pan catches fire, either cover it with a lid or throw bicarbonate of soda or salt on it. Do not blow on it or throw water or flour on it.

If food catches fire in the oven, close the oven door and turn off the heat.

Frozen drains

Put a spoonful of cooking salt down drains last thing at night to prevent them freezing.

Frozen U-trap

If the U-trap under your sink does freeze, thaw it out gradually by wrapping it in cloths wrung out of hot water.

Frying problems

Heat the frying pan before adding butter or oil and the food will not stick.

Sprinkle a little salt in the pan to stop fat spitting.

Add a spoonful of oil to the pan when cooking in butter, to stop the butter burning.

Handles

To avoid accidents, make sure that saucepan handles are turned inwards, and not sticking out, when food is left cooking on the stove.

Hands

If your hands are stained after cleaning or chopping vegetables, rub them with used coffee grounds, or with a cut lemon.

To soften and protect your hands after doing housework, rub them with a teaspoonful each of sugar and cooking oil.

Hot curry

If your curry is too hot, add a small carton of natural yoghurt to calm it down.

Indigestion cure

Pour boiling water over a few sage leaves, leave for five minutes then drink.

Knobs

A missing saucepan lid knob can be replaced by fixing a cork to a screw inserted through the hole.

Lumpy sauce

If a white sauce goes lumpy and you can't get it smooth by beating it hard, strain it through a fine sieve into a clean saucepan.

Rancid butter

Place the butter in a bowl and let it reach room temperature. Add two tablespoons of milk and mix well. Then pour off the excess milk – which will have absorbed the rancid flavour.

Salty potatoes

If boiled potatoes are too salty, mash them with plenty of milk and a beaten egg.

Salty vegetables

If boiled vegetables are too salty, pour boiling water over them.

Grainy yoghurt

Stabilize yoghurt to prevent it separating out in cooking. Mix one teaspoon of cornflour with a little cold water, add this to a small carton of yoghurt and cook gently, stirring all the time, for ten minutes. Then proceed with your recipe.

Snacks and Starters

If your children are perpetually hungry but you hate them eating junk food; if you wake up in the night craving for peanut butter sandwiches or crumpets; if you're short of ideas for quick and original first courses, then here are some hints for you. From toad-in-the-hole to tzatziki, from a *croque monsieur* to a BLT, here are some tantalizing titbits – all made in minutes using basic, wholesome ingredients.

Avocado dip

Blend one ripe avocado with a small carton of sour cream, the juice of half a lemon, salt and freshly ground black pepper to taste. Serve chilled with cut raw vegetables for dipping.

BLT

To make an authentic bacon, lettuce and tomato sandwich, lightly toast two slices of good bread, spread with a tablespoon of mayonnaise, and sandwich together with three crisply fried rashers of bacon, a sliced tomato and some crunchy lettuce leaves.

Cinnamon toast

Sprinkle hot buttered toast with a mixture of half cinnamon and half sugar.

Courgette flowers

Wash and dry the flowers, discard the stamens and dip the flowers in a flour-and-water batter. Fry quickly in deep hot oil until lightly browned.

Home-made crisps

Cut very thin slices of raw potato using a potato peeler or the chisel blade of a grater. Sprinkle with salt and wrap in a clean tea towel to dry for a few minutes, then cook in very hot deep fat. Drain and season to taste.

Croque monsieur

Make sandwiches with a slice each of ham and cheese between buttered bread, and fry in butter until golden brown on both sides.

Home-made crumpets

Heat $\frac{1}{2}$ pint (275 ml) of milk with 4 tablespoons of water until hand-hot, then put into a jug with 1 teaspoon of sugar and 1 tablespoon of dried yeast. Leave in a warm place for 15 minutes until frothy. Sift 8 oz (225 g) of strong plain flour with 1 teaspoon of salt, add the yeast mixture, beat together thoroughly and leave in a warm place for 45 minutes. Grease some metal egg-cooking or pastry-cutting rings, stand them in a hot frying pan and pour a tablespoon of the batter into each one. After 5 minutes, when the holes have formed, remove rings and turn crumpets to cook for 1 minute on the other side. Serve warm at once, or toasted.

Boiled eggs

To prevent eggs cracking when boiling, pierce the shell at the rounded end with a pin. Cook in a small saucepan in water that is simmering gently, not boiling fiercely.

Eggs en cocotte

For 4 people: place 4 ramekin dishes in a large frying pan with water coming halfway up their sides. Put a small knob of butter in each and heat until melted. Divide 2 oz (50 g) of chopped ham or softly fried bacon between them, and crack an egg into each one. Add a tablespoon of double cream, a little salt, freshly ground black pepper and a sprinkling of grated cheese, cover with a lid and cook for about 4 minutes until the whites are barely set (take care not to overcook). Serve with buttered brown bread.

Framed eggs

To make fried eggs more appealing to children, fry a slice of bread on one side, then turn, cut a hole in the middle with a fluted pastry cutter, and crack an egg into this.

Or, place fancy metal pastry or biscuit cutters in the frying pan and simply crack eggs into them to fry in pretty shapes.

Poached eggs

To poach eggs without a poacher, heat water to simmering point in a frying pan (rather than a saucepan). Break eggs gently into it, cook for three minutes, remove and drain.

Flapjacks

Melt 2 oz (50 g) of butter or margarine with 3 tablespoons of golden syrup or brown sugar and mix in 5 oz (150 g) of porridge oats. Spread thinly in a greased baking tin and bake at gas mark 6, 400°F, 200°C for 10 minutes. Cut into portions but cool in tin.

French toast

Beat an egg with three tablespoons of milk, add salt and pepper to taste. Dip three or four slices of bread in the mixture for a few seconds each, then fry golden-brown in butter.

Fried bread

To make your fried bread extra crunchy, moisten the bread slightly before frying. Leftover toast makes particularly good fried bread.

Fried cheese sandwiches

For a tasty, comforting snack, butter one side of a piece of bread and place in a frying pan buttered side down. Spread the top with mayonnaise, then add a generous slice of cheese. Top with another slice of bread, spread on the outside with butter. When the bottom of the sandwich is nicely browned and the cheese is beginning to melt, turn and cook the other side.

Garlic bread

Add chopped fresh herbs to garlic bread to make it even more popular at parties and picnics. For each French loaf, mash together 2 crushed cloves of garlic, 2 tablespoons of chopped mixed herbs (or 2 teaspoons of dried herbs) and 3 oz (75 g) of butter. Insert this in incisions in the loaf at 2-inch (5-cm) intervals, wrap in foil and bake at gas mark 6, 400°F, 200°C for 15 minutes.

Guacamole

For 4 people: mash 2 peeled, ripe avocados with the juice of 1 lemon, 2 peeled and chopped tomatoes, ½ a grated onion, 1 crushed clove of garlic, salt, pepper, a pinch of chilli powder and a dash of Tabasco sauce. Serve soon (otherwise it may go discoloured) with hot crusty bread.

Melba toast

Toast thickly sliced bread slightly on both sides, then remove crusts and cut or pull each in half to make two thin slices. Bake for 2 minutes at gas mark 7, 450°F, 225°C until golden brown and curly. Serve with soup.

Omelette fines herbes

For 2 people: five minutes before you want to eat the omelette, break 4 fresh eggs into a bowl and stir lightly with a fork. Add a little salt and freshly ground black pepper, and half a tablespoon of finely chopped, mixed fresh herbs (preferably parsley, chives, tarragon and chervil). Melt ½ oz (15 g) of butter in a 10-inch (25-cm) omelette pan on the highest possible heat. Just before it colours, tip in the omelette mixture, and add another $\frac{1}{2}$ tablespoon of herbs. Tip and cook the omelette, and when the top is still slightly runny fold it twice and serve at once, topped with a knob of butter. Eat with a crisp green salad and hot fresh bread.

Home-made peanut butter

If you think you don't like peanut butter, it may be because you've only tried the youth hostel sandwich variety. To make it at home, so that it tastes simply delicious (as well as being cheap *and* good for you – peanuts are stuffed with protein), spread a single layer of raw peanuts, skins and all, on a baking tray and roast in a moderate oven, at gas mark 3, 325°F, 170°C, shaking occasionally, until evenly browned (about 15 minutes). Alternatively, cook them when the oven happens to be on for something else. Leave to cool, then grind in the grinder attachment of a blender, add about a teaspoon of salt and a tablespoon of olive oil for every 4 oz (125 g) of peanuts. Store in a screw-top jar – in the fridge, if you can resist eating it all within a week.

Piperade

For 6 people: cook a finely sliced onion in a tablespoon of olive oil or pork dripping in a large pan until it begins to colour, add 6 green peppers cut into strips and cook for 15 minutes more. Then add 2 lb (1 kg) of skinned and chopped tomatoes, 1 chopped clove of garlic, salt, freshly ground black pepper and a pinch of basil. When the tomatoes are tender, add 4 beaten eggs and stir until they begin to scramble. Don't let them solidify, but serve immediately with hot bread.

Poppadums

If fried poppadums fill your kitchen with smoke and still turn out greasy, cook them under the grill instead.

Potted beef

Mince 8 oz (225 g) of leftover cooked beef and cook gently in 1 oz (15 g) of butter with salt, freshly ground pepper, a pinch each of mace and marjoram and a dash of optional brandy for 3 minutes. Press into small pots, cover with a little more melted butter, chill and serve with hot buttered toast.

Roasted seeds

Dry sunflower or pumpkin seeds in the sun, coat with oil and salt, spread on baking sheets and roast at gas mark ½, 250°F, 130°C for 20 minutes. Store in an airtight container. You can eat the seeds whole, or, if you prefer, crack them open and eat only the kernels.

Sandwiches

Soften hard butter for easier spreading by placing a hot pan or bowl upside down over the butter dish for a minute.

Smoked mackerel pâté

For 4 people: skin and flake 1 smoked filleted mackerel. Liquidize it with 2 oz (50 g) of cottage cheese, half a small carton of sour cream, the juice of quarter of a lemon, some salt and freshly ground black pepper. Serve with hot toast and lemon wedges.

Taramasalata

For 6 people: soak 3 crustless slices of white bread in milk for 10 minutes, then put in mixing bowl or blender together with 4 oz (125 g) of smoked cod's roe (skin and all), 1 crushed clove of garlic, 2 tablespoons of single cream, 1 tablespoon of lemon juice and some freshly ground black pepper. Pound or blend until smooth, then slowly add $\frac{1}{3}$ pint (200 ml) of olive oil until the mixture is creamy. Chill and serve with hot toast, lemon wedges and black olives.

Toad-in-the-hole

Sift 4 oz (125 g) of plain flour with $\frac{1}{2}$ teaspoon of salt, break an egg into a well in the centre and start to work in the flour with a fork, gradually adding $\frac{1}{4}$ pint (150 ml) each of milk and water until the batter is smooth. Put 1 lb (450 g) of skinless sausages into a greased baking tin, or individual patty tins, pour the batter over them and bake at gas mark 7, 425°F, 220°C, for about 40 minutes, until risen and golden.

Toast

To avoid tearing freshly made toast by spreading it with hard butter, melt some butter in a pan and dip the toast in it for a second.

Tzatziki

For 6 people: peel and grate a cucumber, stir into 1 pint (575 ml) of natural yoghurt, add a tablespoon each of lemon juice and olive oil, a crushed clove of garlic and a pinch of salt. Serve chilled, and eat with spoons.

Welsh rarebit

For 4 people: heat together 8 oz (225 g) of grated Cheddar, 4 tablespoons of brown ale, 1 oz (25 g) of butter, 1 level teaspoon of dry mustard, a little salt and pepper, until the mixture is hot and creamy. Pour on to 4 slices of toast and grill until golden.

Simple Soups

You may think of soup as the domain of only the most dedicated cook, sweating proudly over a slowly simmering pan. You may think that, unless it comes out of a packet or a tin, soup is bound to take hours, and that its ingredients will need to be carefully planned. But this chapter is designed to change your mind. You can run up a soup in five minutes. You can make it out of the most basic, most surprising things (such as lettuce leaves, pea pods, peanuts, or cheese). So if you're cooking for guests, a home-made soup is an easy way to make an impressive start. And if you're cooking for a family, soup-making can actually save time: any of the following recipes, served with hot crusty bread and followed by fruit and cheese, will make a meal in itself for lunch or supper.

Some general hints: any cream soup will taste more luxurious if you enrich it at the last minute like this. Beat an egg yolk (or two) with a small carton of single cream, then add a few drops of the hot soup, whisking all the time. After you have added about a cupful of soup, return the cream mixture to the soup pan, stir (do not allow to boil, or the cream will curdle) and serve at once.

If your soup is too thin, add a tablespoon of ground rice and whisk. Repeat if necessary. *Or*, if it is a clear soup, blend a tablespoon of arrowroot with a tablespoon of cold water and add this to the soup.

To thicken creamy soups, blend a tablespoon of plain flour with a tablespoon of softened butter and whisk this paste into the soup. Bring back to the boil and cook for two minutes before serving.

Finally, I would point out that although many of the following recipes call for a liquidizer, this isn't absolutely essential: you can often use a potato masher or a sieve, instead. In fact, although a liquidizer is the one kitchen gadget I wouldn't be without, I think too many smooth soups can easily get monotonous. So, for the sake of variety, serve some rough, chunky soups now and then.

See also salad soup (page 35), potato and onion soup (page 94) and storecupboard standby soups (pages 81–5).

Avocado soup

For 4 people: peel and chop 2 avocados, and blend with 1½ pints (875 ml) of chicken stock. Add a small carton of single cream, salt and freshly ground black pepper and either chill or heat to serve.

Bortsch

For 4 people: peel and shred 1 large beetroot and cook gently in 2 oz (50 g) of butter in a covered saucepan for 20 minutes. Meanwhile dilute a 15-oz (425-g) tin of beef consommé according to directions, add to the beetroot and cook for 20 minutes more. Sieve or blend, reheat, season to taste, and serve with a spoonful of sour cream and a sprinkling of freshly chopped chives in each bowl.

Carrot soup

For 4 people: sauté 1 lb (450 g) of chopped carrots with 1 chopped onion in 2 oz (50 g) of butter for 5 minutes. Add 2 pints (1 litre) of chicken stock, a pinch each of sugar and mace, and simmer for 20 minutes. Purée in a blender, then reheat, seasoning to taste. Garnish with chopped chives.

Cheese soup

For 6 people: soften 2 chopped potatoes, 2 chopped onions, 1 chopped carrot and 1 chopped stick of celery in 2 oz (50 g) of butter for 5 minutes. Add 1½ pints (875 ml) of chicken stock and simmer for 15 minutes, then add 4 oz (125 g) of grated Cheddar, seasoning, and 3 tablespoons of single cream or top of the milk. When the cheese has melted, sprinkle with paprika and serve.

Courgette soup

For 4 people: simmer 1½ lb (675 g) of chopped courgettes in 1 pint (575 ml) of chicken stock for 6 minutes. Blend and reheat, adding more stock to thin if you wish, a small carton of single cream, salt and freshly ground black pepper.

Cucumber and yoghurt soup

For 5 people: peel and dice 1 medium cucumber, sprinkle with salt and leave to drain for half an hour. Rinse and dry. Rub a large bowl with a cut garlic clove, then combine in it the cucumber with 1 pint (575 ml) each of fresh natural yoghurt and iced water, and 2 crushed cloves of garlic. Beat in 2 tablespoons of olive oil, chill and season to taste with salt, pepper and a dash of lemon juice before serving.

Egg and lemon soup

For 5 people: bring 2 pints (1 litre) of home-made chicken stock to the boil and add 2 oz (50 g) of uncooked long grain rice. Simmer until the rice is tender (or use leftover cooked rice) and season with salt and pepper. Beat 2 eggs together with the juice of half a lemon, gradually add a cupful of the hot broth to this, beating all the time, then return it to the pan and heat gently until almost but not quite boiling.

Fish chowder

For 6 people: get the fishmonger to skin and fillet 2 lb (1 kg) of white fish – cod, haddock or whiting – for you, but keep all the bones, heads and skin. Simmer them in 1 pint (575 ml) of water for 20 minutes to make stock, then strain. Meanwhile, soften 2 chopped rashers of streaky bacon, then add 1 sliced onion, 1 lb (450 g) of chopped potatoes, 1 pint (575 ml) of milk, the fish stock and the flaked fish. Simmer for 15 minutes, then season generously with salt, pepper and lemon juice, and garnish with fresh chopped parsley.

Herb soup

For 4 people: soften 2 tablespoons of chopped spring onions with 2 large peeled and chopped potatoes in 2 oz (50 g) of butter for 5 minutes. Add the washed and shredded outer leaves of a large lettuce and 1 pint (575 ml) of chicken stock, and simmer for 10 minutes. Purée in a blender with 2 heaped tablespoons of chopped mixed herbs (such as parsley, mint, sage, thyme, chervil, etc.), and a small carton of single cream. Reheat gently, seasoning with salt, pepper and lemon juice.

Jerusalem artichoke soup

For 4 people: sauté 1 lb (450 g) of peeled and chopped Jerusalem artichokes in 2 oz (50 g) butter for 5 minutes, then simmer in 1 pint (575 ml) of chicken stock for 15 minutes. Purée in a liquidizer, then reheat, adding salt, freshly ground black pepper and a small carton of single cream.

Leek and potato soup

For 4 people: soften the chopped white of 4 leeks with 4 chopped potatoes in 2 oz (50 g) of butter. Add 1½ pints (875 ml) of chicken stock and simmer for 15 minutes. Mash slightly to break up the potatoes, season with salt and black pepper, and sprinkle with chopped fresh parsley to serve.

Lettuce soup

For 4 people: shred the leaves of 2 large whole lettuces, or the outer leaves of 3, and simmer in 1 pint (575 ml) of chicken stock for 10 minutes. Purée in a blender, return to the pan, add a small carton of single cream or a knob of butter, and season with salt, freshly ground black pepper, a pinch of sugar and a sprinkling of fresh nutmeg.

Pea soup

For 4 people: soften 1 chopped onion in 2 oz (50 g) butter for 5 minutes, then add 1 lb (450 g) fresh or frozen peas and 1 pint (575 ml) chicken stock. Simmer for 10 minutes, then purée in a blender and reheat, seasoning to taste with a pinch of sugar, salt, freshly ground black pepper, and adding a few tablespoons of top-of-the-milk or single cream

Pea pod soup

For 4 people: simmer 1 lb (450 g) of tender young green pea pods with 1 chopped onion, 1 chopped carrot and 1 chopped stick of celery in ½ pint (275 ml) of water for half an hour. Blend in a liquidizer, then thin with up to 1 pint (575 ml) of chicken stock to make a deliciously creamy soup.

Peanut soup

For 6 people: roast 4 oz (125 g) of shelled peanuts at gas mark 3, 325°F, 170°C for 15 minutes. Make 2 pints (1 litre) of chicken stock, put the nuts in a blender with just enough stock to cover, and purée. Transfer to a heavy pan with the rest of the stock, cover, and simmer for 15 minutes. Season with salt and freshly ground black pepper, and stir in a small carton of single cream and a dash of dry sherry just before serving.

Cold tomato soup

For 4 people: purée 3 lb (1·5 kg) of skinned fresh or tinned tomatoes and sieve to remove pips. Add a pinch of sugar, the juice and grated zest of a lemon, salt, freshly ground black pepper, some chopped fresh basil and a small carton of single cream. Serve chilled.

Fish, Poultry and Meat

Meat is so expensive now that it makes sense to follow these rules.

1. *Make sure you get your money's worth.* Choose a butcher who clearly has a rapid turnover, who offers a wide variety of meat, and whose meat looks fresh. Avoid shops that have rose-tinted fluorescent lighting which is designed to make the meat look redder. If you can find a butcher who is also knowledgeable – who can advise you on what is good value at the moment, and how different cuts of meat

need to be cooked – you are in luck; and if you find one who is also obliging – who is prepared to mince and chop and bone and roll meat for you specially – then don't ever leave him.

2. *Treat meat with care.* Don't just stick it in the oven and forget it. Follow recipes attentively, washing and drying and seasoning and basting according to instructions. Don't lose precious juices by prodding or lifting lids or carving too soon; don't overcook it; and don't drown it in over-powering sauces.

3. *Don't waste any.* Buy large joints when you can and you'll be surprised how far they stretch. They are certainly more economical than chops and steaks. You probably have your own favourite recipes for leftover meat (see also rissoles, page 35, and meatballs, page 33). But don't forget to use the bones to make stock (page 111), and the dripping for roasting potatoes and frying other vegetables.

4. *Be adventurous.* Why not, for example, try every kind of meat, in turn, that the butcher has to offer? (This is a wonderful plan if you hate thinking up menus.) In particular, experiment with offal. Not only does it present a whole range of different flavours and texture, but offal is also relatively cheap, extremely nutritious, and in many cases quick to cook.

Fish

Anchovies

Soak anchovies in milk for an hour or so before using to absorb saltiness.

Cod's roe

To prepare raw cod's roe, wrap in foil or muslin and put in a pan of simmering salted water with a dash of vinegar added. Cook gently for thirty minutes, then cool. Remove skin just before using.

Grilled fish

If you make slashes about one inch (3 cm) apart in the skin on both sides of a fish (such as mackerel or herring) before placing it under the grill, it will cook more quickly and evenly.

To bone a herring

Cut along the stomach and open the fish out flat. Lay the cut side down on a chopping board and rub your finger firmly all along the backbone. Turn the fish over and you will now be able to remove the bones easily.

Kippers

To minimize the smell of cooking kippers, wrap them in foil and cook in the oven, or cook them in a covered pan of boiling water.

Jugged kippers

Put kippers into a tall jug, cover with boiling water and leave for five minutes. Drain and serve.

Lobsters

You can tell a fresh lobster by its stiff tail.

Poultry

To draw poultry

Cut off the feet and draw the sinews in the legs, then cut off the head and neck and loosen the gullet and windpipe. Remove the entrails through the tail end vent, reserving the heart, gizzard and liver (not the yellow gall bladder) for making stock. Wash the cavity.

To pluck poultry

Start at the breast and work towards the head. Then pluck the back and the wings. Take out two or three feathers at a time by pulling sharply in the opposite direction to the way they lie. Singe remaining small feathers and hairs with a taper, then wipe with a damp cloth.

Roasting poultry

Don't forget to season the cavity of the bird before roasting, as well as the skin.

Stuffing poultry

To stuff the breast, loosen the flap of skin at the neck end of the bird to make a pocket between the breast and skin. Insert about a third of the stuffing here. Do not overfill, as the stuffing will expand during cooking. Fold back the neck flap to cover the opening and fasten with a meat skewer. Place the rest of the stuffing inside the body cavity.

Fried chicken

Fried chicken is actually better baked. Toss chicken portions in seasoned flour and brown quickly in butter. Transfer to a roasting tin and cook skin side up, at gas mark 4, 350°F, 180°C for 45 minutes, basting occasionally.

Peking Duck

The secret of a really crisp Peking Duck is to dry the skin thoroughly before cooking. You can do this by hanging it up near a heater overnight, or, if you're in a hurry, dry it by hand with a hairdryer for fifteen minutes.

Roast duck

A duck is a fatty bird, so do not add any butter or oil to it before roasting. Instead, prick the flesh deeply all over with a skewer to allow some of the fat to escape during cooking. Roast on a rack. Afterwards, keep the fat and use it for roasting potatoes.

Leftover turkey

For a delicious and unusual post-Christmas treat, carve some thin, broad slices of turkey breast and place on each one a generous spoonful of good home-made stuffing, plenty of chopped fresh parsley and a little chopped garlic. Roll up (against the grain, to avoid splitting) and fry rapidly in butter for 3 minutes.

Meat

Salty bacon

If bacon rashers are too salty, soak them in warm water for fifteen minutes and dry on kitchen towels before cooking.

If a joint of bacon has been powerfully salted (ask your butcher), it should be soaked overnight in cold water before cooking. The next day, bring it to the boil in the soaking liquid, drain and rinse off the scum in cold water. Then continue cooking.

If you add a peeled potato to the water when boiling a joint of bacon it will absorb some excess saltiness.

Bacon rinds

Render the delicious fat from bacon rinds by heating them gently in a frying pan or a slow oven. Strain the fat and it can be kept for up to two weeks in the refrigerator and used for frying.

Or, fry bacon rinds until crisp and curly to serve for nibbling.

Beating

When beating out meat to tenderize it (use a rolling pin if you haven't got a bat), sprinkle a little water on both the work surface and the rolling pin so that the meat will not stick to either.

Browning

When searing meat before putting it into a casserole, it is best to cook only a few pieces at a time, in a single layer. If you overcrowd the pan the meat will take longer to heat up, and will remain soft instead of forming a firm outer coating.

Carving roasts

A roast should be left to stand on a hot dish at room temperature for at least twenty minutes before carving, so that the juices (which rise to the surface during cooking) have time to retreat back into the meat. Don't worry: it really won't get cold!

Crackling

For success with crackling, make sure that the skin of the pork joint is absolutely dry before you put it in the oven. Do not put any fat on it, only a little salt; and cook it in a shallow roasting tin so that the skin is fully exposed to the heat of the oven.

To make crackling extra crisp, mix the juice of one lemon with an equal amount of boiling water, pour this over the joint 10 minutes before the end of the cooking time, and put back in the oven turned up to gas mark 8, 450°F, 230°C.

Gammon steaks

Nick the edges of a gammon steak with a sharp knife before cooking, to prevent it curling.

Garlic in roasts

When roasting meat with slivers of garlic in it, make sure that the garlic is completely buried in the flesh, otherwise it will burn and smell – and taste – bitter.

Grilling

Put a piece of stale bread in the grill pan when grilling meat to soak up the dripping fat and stop it smoking or catching fire.

Boiled ham

If you are going to eat boiled ham cold, let it cool in the cooking water and it will be juicier.

Salty ham

Over-salty slices of cooked ham can be soaked in milk for half an hour, then rinsed in cold water.

Perfect hamburgers

Use only the best mince: hamburgers should be very lean.
For two generous hamburgers, mix 1 lb (450 g) of mince with
salt, freshly ground black pepper, 1 teaspoon of made
mustard, 1 beaten egg, and a dash of tomato ketchup or
mayonnaise (not salad cream). Mould by hand into two flat
cakes and refrigerate for half an hour at least. Heat a little
oil in a frying pan until very hot and smoking, then cook
the hamburgers for 2 or 3 minutes on each side, or more if
you like them well done.

If you have to cook a lot of hamburgers in a short time,
make a dent in the middle of each one to allow the heat to
penetrate faster.

Kidneys

To prepare kidneys for cooking, remove the transparent
skin, then snip out the core with kitchen scissors. You may
find it easier to slice the kidney lengthwise first to get at the
core more easily.

Roast lamb

Lamb should always be served on very hot plates, so that
its fat will not congeal.

Larding

To keep large joints of lean meat or large game birds moist
while roasting, thread narrow strips of fat through the flesh
about ¼ inch (0·5 cm) deep at regular intervals all over
the surface, using a special larding needle.

Liver

Soak liver in milk for half an hour before cooking to make
it particularly tender.

If you need to cut raw liver into thin slices, pour boiling water over it, leave for one minute, then drain. It will now be easier to cut.

Roast pork

When carving roast pork, remove a wide section of crackling first so that the meat will be easier to slice. Then divide the crackling into individual portions.

To make a change from apple sauce when serving roast pork, core some eating apples, slice (do not peel them) and fry gently in butter until tender.

Smoother pork

Pour boiling water over a joint of pork or pig's trotters before cooking to clean the flesh and make it easier to remove hairs.

Roasting rack

Instead of a metal rack, roast your meat on a bed of chopped vegetables – onion, carrot and celery. This has the same effect of allowing heat to circulate all round the meat while it is cooking; and afterwards you can mash the vegetables into the pan juices to add extra flavour to your gravy.

Seasoning

Don't sprinkle salt on meat before grilling or roasting it, because salt encourages the juices to escape. Season it at the last minute, just before serving.

Stuffing

If you soak breadcrumbs in water or milk before adding them to the stuffing mixture you will not need so many eggs to bind it.

Sweetbreads

To prepare sweetbreads for cooking, soak in cold water for 1–2 hours, then drain, cover with fresh cold water in a saucepan, add the juice of half a lemon, bring to the boil and simmer for 5 minutes. Drain and cool, then remove any tough bits of skin and veins.

Meat thermometer

When inserting a meat thermometer in a joint make sure that it is not touching a bone or buried in a thick layer of fat, or its readings will be misleading.

Tongs

It is best to use kitchen tongs rather than a fork to turn steaks and chops. If you pierce meat with a fork some of the delicious juices will escape.

Storecupboard Standbys

For those occasions when guests turn up unannounced and starving, or when the clock stops, or you forget it's a Bank Holiday and miss the shops, or when you actually find something more interesting to do all day than visit the butcher and the greengrocer – here are some suggestions. Of course, if you have a freezer, in theory you should never have to face such crises. But aren't there days when you forget to get things out to thaw?

For a start, as long as you have a packet of spaghetti in the cupboard, and some Parmesan cheese (preferably in a

lump, so that you can grate it freshly yourself), and butter
and salt and black pepper, you need never be at a loss. (Toss
the cooked spaghetti in a generous knob of butter in the
pan and serve very hot scattered with cheese and pepper.)
And if you always have eggs at hand, there's bound to be
something in the fridge that you can stick inside a fluffy
omelette.

But to be more systematic about it, always try to keep at
least some of the things listed below in your storecupboard,
so that you can relax in the knowledge that you have several
substantial meals in there, just waiting to be thrown together.

Tins

anchovies
crab, prawns or shrimps
frankfurters
beans (haricot, kidney)
mushrooms
tomatoes
tuna

Dried goods

flour
haricot beans
lentils
macaroni
spaghetti
split peas
sugar

Frozen

bread dough
chicken livers
peas
spinach

Fresh

bacon
butter
carrots
celery
cheese (cheddar, Parmesan)
eggs
garlic
lemons
milk
oil
onions
potatoes

Flavourings

basil
bay leaves
black pepper
chicken stock cubes
cloves
nutmeg
parsley
salt
tomato purée

Bacon, beans and rice

For 4 people: cook a crushed clove of garlic, a finely chopped onion and 4 oz (125 g) of chopped streaky bacon in a tablespoon of olive oil until tender but not browned, then add a small tin of chopped tomatoes, salt, freshly ground black pepper and a pinch of sugar. Simmer for 15 minutes, then add a tinful of cooked red kidney beans, a mugful of uncooked long grain rice, and a mugful of hot chicken stock. Cover and simmer for 20 minutes or until the rice is tender, adding more stock if necessary. Just before serving, add a handful of chopped fresh parsley.

Bean and pasta soup

For 4 people: soften a chopped onion and a crushed clove of garlic in olive oil, add 2 tablespoons of tomato purée and a pinch of dried or fresh chopped basil, 8 oz (225 g) of cooked haricot beans and 1 pint (575 ml) of chicken stock. Simmer for half an hour, then purée half of the soup. Return this to the pan with the rest and add 4 oz (125 g) of short macaroni. Simmer for 10 minutes, then serve with plenty of freshly grated Parmesan.

Chicken liver risotto

For 3 people: soften a sliced onion and 2 oz (50 g) of chopped bacon in 1 oz (25 g) of butter, then add 8 oz (225 g) of thawed frozen chicken livers and brown lightly. Add a small tin of mushrooms, $\frac{1}{2}$ pint (275 ml) of chicken stock, 1 bay leaf, 1 tablespoon of tomato purée, a pinch of dried basil, salt and pepper. Cook for 10 minutes. Meanwhile in a separate pan soften 1 chopped onion in butter, stir in a mugful of uncooked rice and cook until transparent. Add 2 mugfuls of chicken stock and cook until the rice is tender. Season and serve together with the sauce and plenty of freshly grated Parmesan.

Eggs Florentine

For 4 people: prepare a 1 lb (450 g) packet of frozen spinach according to the directions, season with salt, pepper and freshly grated nutmeg, and place in a buttered ovenproof dish. Crack 4 eggs into depressions in the spinach, season, and cover with cheese sauce made with 2 oz (50 g) each of butter and flour, 1 pint (575 ml) of milk, and 4 oz (125 g) of grated cheese. Bake at gas mark 5, 375°F, 190°C for 15 minutes.

Fish and potato soup

For 4 people: peel and roughly chop 1 lb (450 g) of potatoes and 1 onion. Cook gently in 1 tablespoon of butter until soft, then add 1½ pints (875 ml) of milk, and salt and pepper, and simmer for 20 minutes. Purée in a blender, then reheat, adding 4 oz (125 g) of flaked tinned tuna or salmon and a small carton of single cream or the top of a pint of milk.

Frankfurters

Put frankfurters in a pan of boiling water, cover, remove from heat and leave for 5 minutes. Drain and serve with hot or cold potato salad (page 92).

Lentil soup

For 6 people: wash 6 oz (175 g) of brown lentils – they don't need soaking – and put them in a large pan with 2½ pints (2·25 litres) of stock, 1 crushed clove of garlic, 2 large chopped onions, 6 oz (175 g) chopped bacon, 1 small tin of tomatoes, and 1 clove. Bring to the boil, cover and simmer for 1 hour, then add 1 lb (450 g) of chopped potatoes and cook for 20 minutes more. Remove the clove, purée the soup and reheat it, adding 2 tablespoons each of lemon juice and chopped parsley just before serving. Serve with hot bread and a green salad.

Split pea soup

For 4 people: simmer 8 oz (225 g) of split peas – they don't need soaking – in 2 pints (1 litre) of chicken stock for 30 minutes. Soften 1 chopped onion, 1 chopped carrot, 1 chopped celery stalk and a handful of chopped bacon in butter, then add this to the peas and simmer for 45 minutes more. Purée in a liquidizer, reheat, season, and stir in a knob of butter before serving.

Pizza

For 4 people: roll out a packet of frozen bread dough into a large round and leave on a greased baking sheet in a warm place to prove. Soften 1 large chopped onion and 1 chopped garlic clove in 1 tablespoon of olive oil, add a 14-oz (400-g) tin of tomatoes, 1 tablespoon of tomato purée and 1 teaspoon of dried basil. Simmer for half an hour. Spread this over the dough base, then cover with a layer of chopped tinned mushrooms, thinly sliced cheese and a small tin of anchovies. Sprinkle with olive oil and any chopped fresh herbs you have, and bake at gas mark 7, 425°F, 220°C for 20 minutes.

Rice and peas

For 2 people: soften 1 chopped onion in butter, then add 2 oz (50 g) chopped bacon or ham and an 8-oz (225-g) packet of frozen peas. Add ½ pint (275 ml) chicken stock and 8 oz (225 g) of long grain rice. Simmer for 20 minutes, adding another ½ pint (275 ml) of chicken stock as the liquid is absorbed. Season and serve with freshly grated Parmesan.

Seafood pancakes

For 4 people: make pancakes using 4 oz (125 g) of plain flour, 1 egg, ¼ pint (150 ml) each of milk and water, and seasoning. Cook and keep warm over a pan of hot water.

For the filling, make a white sauce using 1 oz (25 g) each of butter and flour and ½ pint (275 ml) of milk. Add a small tin of crabmeat, a 7-oz (200-g) tin of prawns or shrimps and a 7-oz (200-g) tin of mushrooms, all drained, together with 1 tablespoon of lemon juice and 3 tablespoons of single cream or top-of-the-milk. Heat thoroughly, then fill the pancakes and serve at once.

Seafood quiche

For 4 people: soften 2 tablespoons of finely chopped onion in butter, then add 4 oz (125 g) tinned crab or shrimps or lobster, or a combination of these. Stir and cook gently for 2 minutes, add salt, pepper and 2 tablespoons of vermouth or white wine or chicken stock, boil for 1 minute and cool. Meanwhile beat 3 eggs with a small carton of single cream or ¼ pint (150 ml) of top-of-the-milk or milk. Blend in 1 tablespoon of tomato purée, season with salt and pepper, then add the shellfish mixture. Pour into an 8-inch (20-cm) partly cooked pastry case, dot with grated cheese, and bake at gas mark 5, 375°F, 190°C for 30 minutes until risen and golden.

Spaghetti carbonara

For 4 people: chop 8 oz (225 g) bacon or ham and sauté in butter. Beat 4 eggs lightly with seasoning and a small carton of single cream or ¼ pint (150 ml) of top-of-the-milk or milk. Cook 1 lb (450 g) of spaghetti until *al dente*, drain, and combine all ingredients in a large warmed bowl. Serve at once with freshly grated Parmesan and lots of black pepper.

Spaghetti with chicken livers

For 4 people: soften 1 chopped onion in olive oil, then add 12 oz (350 g) defrosted frozen chicken livers and sauté for

5 minutes. Add a small tin of mushrooms, a 14-oz (400-g) tin of tomatoes, 1 tablespoon of tomato purée, and simmer for 20 minutes. Season with salt and pepper, and add a tablespoon of chopped parsley just before serving with spaghetti and Parmesan.

Spaghetti with clams

For 4 people: soften 1 finely chopped onion in olive oil, then add 2 crushed cloves of garlic, and a 14-oz (400-g) tin of tomatoes. Simmer for 20 minutes, then add 12 oz (350 g) tinned clams, 2 tablespoons of chopped parsley, salt, pepper and, if you like it, a pinch of dried red chilli peppers. Serve with 1 lb (450 g) of spaghetti, and *no* Parmesan.

Spaghetti with mushrooms and peas

For 2 people: soften 1 chopped onion in butter, add 2 oz (50 g) of chopped bacon, a 4-oz (125-g) packet of frozen peas and a small tin of mushrooms. When hot, season with plenty of black pepper and serve with spaghetti and Parmesan.

Spinach soup

For 4 people: make a white sauce using 1 oz (25 g) each of butter and flour and ½ pint (275 ml) of milk. Add ½ pint (275 ml) of chicken stock and an 8-oz (225-g) packet or tin of spinach. When hot, season with salt, pepper and freshly grated nutmeg.

Tuna and bean salad

For 4 people: combine 1 lb (450 g) of cooked white haricot beans with 1 sliced raw onion, 8 oz (225 g) of tinned tuna, salt, freshly ground black pepper and plenty of olive oil.

Tunafish cocktail

For 4 people: flake an 8-oz (225-g) tin of tuna and sprinkle with lemon juice and black pepper. Mix ½ pint (275 ml) of mayonnaise with 1 tablespoon each of single cream or top-of-the-milk and tomato purée. Arrange the fish on beds of shredded lettuce in individual dishes, cover with the sauce and garnish with lemon slices.

Potatoes

This chapter is designed to dispel any notion you may ever have had about potatoes being boring. Not only does it suggest ways of preparing and cooking them more quickly and more efficiently, so as to get all possible goodness out of them (the best news as far as I'm concerned is that it's better not to peel them, because their vitamins are concentrated just under the skin). Not only does it suggest ways of making a tasty, nutritious and economical meal out of little more than a potato, and of improving your chips; it also includes some hints from the Scots, Irish, French,

Italians, Americans, Swedes, Jews, Germans and Russians on how to make the most of this underrated vegetable.

Aligot (*French*)

For 6 people: boil 2 lb (1 kg) of floury potatoes in their skins, then peel them and mash or purée. Add salt and pepper. Heat 2 oz (50 g) of butter with a small carton of single cream gently in a heavy pan, blend in the potato purée, then add a crushed clove of garlic and 8 oz (225 g) of grated cheese. Stir until the mixture is smooth, then serve at once with a crisp green salad.

Baked potatoes

Smear the skins of jacket potatoes with oil before cooking to make them crisp and delicious.

Potatoes will bake faster with skewers or nails stuck in them.

Bubble and squeak

Mix leftover mashed potato with leftover cooked cabbage (or parsnip, carrot or celery) and seasoning. Heat butter, dripping or oil in a frying pan, add vegetable mixture, flatten and fry, turning once, until golden on both sides.

Chips

Perfect chips are cooked in two stages. First cut the potatoes and dry them thoroughly on a clean tea towel or on kitchen paper. Heat fat or oil at first to 350°F, 180°C (at which temperature a cube of bread will turn golden brown in 1 minute). Put chips in frying basket and cook steadily until tender but not coloured. Now remove them and keep them warm while heating the fat or oil to 390°F, 195°C (at this temperature a cube of bread will brown in ½ minute). Return

the chips to the pan and fry quickly until crisp and golden.
Drain and season.

Colcannon (*Irish*)

For 4 people: soften a chopped onion in 2 oz (50 g) of bacon
fat, then add 1 lb (450 g) of mashed potatoes and 8 oz (225 g)
of cooked shredded cabbage. Season generously, transfer to
a greased pudding basin and bake at gas mark 5, 375°F,
190°C for 20 minutes. Turn out on to a serving dish.

Potato croquettes

For 4 people: beat an egg and use half of it to bind 1 lb
(450 g) of well-seasoned mashed potatoes. With floured
hands shape the mixture into sausage shapes, dip in the rest
of the beaten egg and then in breadcrumbs. Fry in hot deep
fat until golden brown.

Farmhouse supper

For 4 people: soften 8 oz (225 g) of chopped streaky bacon
in a frying pan until the fat runs, then remove bacon and put
1 lb (450 g) of chopped cooked potatoes and a finely chopped
onion in the pan to brown lightly. Season, add the bacon,
and transfer to an ovenproof dish. Put 4 lightly fried eggs
on top, sprinkle with 4 oz (125 g) grated cheese, and place
under the grill for 1 minute before serving.

Potato gnocchi (*Italian*)

For 4 people: mix 1 lb (450 g) leftover mashed potato with
a beaten egg, a tablespoon of melted butter and 4 tablespoons of flour (either kind) to make a mouldable dough.
(Add more flour if necessary.) Roll into a 1-inch (3-cm) wide
sausage, then chop up and roll in the palms of your hands
into 1-inch (3-cm) balls, and drop into a large pan of boiling

water to poach for 3 minutes, or until the gnocchi rise to the surface. Drain and serve with butter or with fresh tomato sauce (page 116), and freshly grated Parmesan.

Hashed brown potatoes (*American*)

For 4 people: melt 2 tablespoons of pork dripping or chopped salt pork, then add 1½ lb (675 g) of finely chopped cold boiled potatoes. Mix thoroughly and add seasoning to taste. Cook gently until brown underneath, then fold in half like an omelette to serve.

Home fries (*American*)

For 4 people: melt 2 tablespoons of margarine or butter in a heavy frying pan, arrange 1½ lb (675 g) of peeled and thinly sliced potatoes in the pan in two or three layers, sprinkling each layer with salt and pepper and dotting with more margarine or butter. Cover and cook for 15 minutes, then uncover and cook, turning occasionally, until tender, crisp and brown all over. Add a little chopped onion if you wish.

Janssons temptation (*Swedish*)

For 4 people: chop 1 lb (450 g) of raw peeled potatoes into matchsticks and arrange half in a buttered ovenproof dish. Spread with 2 large onions cut into rings and softened in butter, and a drained tin of anchovy fillets. Season with pepper, but not salt. Add the rest of the potatoes, dot with butter, pour on half a small carton of single cream and bake at gas mark 7, 425°F, 220°C, until the top is golden brown. Pour on the rest of the cream, reduce heat to gas mark 5, 375°F, 190°C and continue cooking until the potatoes are tender (about 45 minutes in all). Sprinkle with chopped fresh parsley and serve hot.

Latkes (*Jewish*)

For 4 people: peel 1 lb (450 g) of potatoes, soak in cold water for half an hour, then grate into a mixing bowl. Add 1 tablespoon of flour, 1 beaten egg, a little grated onion, and seasoning. Heat some oil or dripping in a frying pan and drop the mixture in one tablespoonful at a time. Flatten, and fry, turning once, until golden on both sides. Serve alone as a snack, or to accompany meat or, omitting the onion, with apple sauce, jam or sour cream.

Mashed potatoes

Make mashed potatoes extra good by mixing with sour cream instead of milk, and adding freshly grated nutmeg.
 Or, mix with hot milk instead of cold.

New potatoes

Bring the water to the boil before adding the potatoes – so that they are in the water for the shortest possible time, and will lose less flavour.

Oven-fried potatoes

For 4 people: pre-heat oven to gas mark 5, 375°F, 190°C, and place a tablespoon of dripping in a baking tin to melt. Peel 1 lb (450 g) of old potatoes and cut into ⅓-inch (1-cm) slices. Toss them in the dripping and cook for 40 minutes or until crisp and golden.

Pan Haggerty (*Northern English*)

For 4 people: peel and boil 1½ lb (675 g) of potatoes and cut into thin slices. Soften 2 chopped onions in 2 oz (50 g) of dripping in a heavy frying pan, remove and drain. Then in the same pan arrange the potatoes, onions and 4 oz (125 g) of grated cheese in layers, seasoning generously with salt and freshly ground black pepper. Cover and cook gently for 20 minutes, then brown under the grill.

Potato pancakes (*Scottish*)

For 4 people: purée 8 oz (225 g) boiled potatoes with 2 eggs, 6 oz (175 g) of flour, 1 pint (575 ml) of milk, salt and pepper. Using a tablespoon of the mixture for each pancake, cook in dripping for 1 minute on each side. Serve hot, with butter and honey for tea, or with bacon for breakfast.

Parsleyed potatoes

For 4 people: sauté 1½ lb (675 g) of peeled and chopped potatoes in butter, then cover with half milk and half water. Simmer for 25 minutes, then add a handful of finely chopped parsley and cook for 5 minutes more, until the liquid is almost entirely absorbed.

Potato salad (*German*)

For 4 people: wash 1½ lb (450 g) of old potatoes, put in a pan of boiling salted water to cover, and cook until just tender. Drain, cut into slices, put in a mixing bowl and stir in 4 tablespoons of hot chicken stock. After 5 minutes add some vinaigrette dressing (page 101), and a little chopped onion if you like, toss thoroughly, sprinkle with freshly chopped parsley or chives, and serve warm or cold.

Quick sauté potatoes

For 4 people: peel 1½ lb (675 g) of old potatoes and parboil for 10 minutes. Drain and slice thinly. Heat 2 tablespoons of olive oil in a heavy frying pan and cook the potatoes quickly, in a single layer, for 5 minutes on each side, or until golden brown and crisp. (To save time, use two frying pans.) Remove, drain on kitchen paper, season and serve at once.

Rösti (Swiss)

For 4 people: peel 1 lb (450 g) of leftover jacket potatoes. (If you haven't any, parboil potatoes in their skins, then peel.) Slice thinly and season. Heat 2 oz (50 g) butter or dripping in a frying pan and fry the potatoes until golden brown. Reduce heat, press the potatoes into a cake, add 2 tablespoons of water, cover and cook for 15 minutes more. Turn upside down to serve.

Russian potatoes

For 4 people: boil 4 large potatoes in their skins until they are barely cooked. Peel and cube them, and mix with 6 oz (150 g) of cottage cheese, 1 tablespoon of plain yoghurt, 2 tablespoons of chopped onion or spring onion, and 1 crushed clove of garlic. Season with salt and pepper, put into a buttered dish and sprinkle 3 oz (75 g) of grated Cheddar cheese over the top. Bake at gas mark 5, 375°F, 190°C for half an hour.

Potato scones (Scottish)

For 4 people: mash 1 lb (450 g) of boiled old potatoes together with 2 level teaspoons of salt, 2 oz (50 g) of butter, and 4 oz (125 g) of flour. Knead lightly on a floured board, roll out to ½ inch (1 cm) thick and cut into triangles. Cook on a hot greased griddle or in a heavy frying pan for 5 minutes on each side until golden brown. Serve hot, with bacon and eggs.

Soufflé potatoes

For 4 people: beat ¼ pint (150 ml) of hot milk or single cream into 1½ lb (675 g) of mashed potatoes. Add seasoning, 1 tablespoon chopped parsley and 2 egg yolks, then fold in 2 stiffly beaten egg whites and cook in a buttered soufflé dish in a pre-heated oven at gas mark 6, 400°F, 200°C for 30 minutes until risen and browning.

Onion and potato soup

For 4 people: sauté 8 oz (225 g) of chopped onion with 8 oz (225 g) of chopped potato in butter for 5 minutes, until softened and glazed. Add ¼ pint (150 ml) chicken stock, and simmer for 10 minutes until tender. Purée in a liquidizer, adding ½ pint (275 ml) of milk to cool. Reheat, adding more milk to thin the soup to taste (or a small carton of single cream for extra richness), and season with salt and freshly ground black pepper.

Steamed potatoes

Steamed potatoes – like every other vegetable – have far more flavour than boiled. Peel them and place in a colander over a panful of simmering water, add salt, cover with a lid and cook for the usual time until tender.

Stovies (*Scottish*)

For 4 people: soften 2 sliced onions in 2 tablespoons of dripping, then add 1½ lb (675 g) of peeled and sliced potatoes, salt and pepper, and ½ inch (1·5 cm) of water. Cover and cook gently for 30 minutes, shaking occasionally, until the potatoes are tender.

Other Vegetables, and Salads

This chapter offers some suggestions about new ways of cooking familiar vegetables, and some simple ways of cooking strange ones.

In general, be kind to your vegetables, so as to preserve all of their goodness and flavour. Don't overcook them. Steam them rather than boil, so that you don't lose the vitamins that dissolve in water. If you must boil, use very little water, and bring it to the boil first, so that the vegetables are in it for the shortest possible time. And afterwards, save the cooking water (and the peelings) for stocks and soups.

Try to enhance the flavour of vegetables with careful seasoning (see cauliflower au gratin, cabbage with caraway seeds, French-style carrots and peas). Don't smother them with strong sauces. Remember that many vegetables are best appreciated raw – or cooked and cooled – in salads (see leeks vinaigrette, page 99, and three-bean salad, page 101).

Be adventurous: look round street markets to find vegetables you don't know, and discover how to cook them. This is often a simple and inexpensive way of expanding your culinary repertoire.

Artichokes

To prepare artichokes for cooking, remove the stalk from the bottom. (If you wish, pull out the cone of pale thin leaves from the top, and then scoop out the inedible hairy 'choke', using a teaspoon, and sprinkle the cavity with lemon juice to prevent discoloration.)

To cook artichokes, bring a large panful of salted water to the boil (do not use an iron or aluminium pan as this may discolour the artichokes), and add a tablespoon of lemon juice. Boil gently for 30–40 minutes until the bases are tender. Drain thoroughly and serve hot, warm or cold with vinaigrette dressing (page 101), hollandaise sauce (page 145), mayonnaise (page 113) or simply with a mixture of melted butter and lemon juice.

Dried beans

When cooking dried beans, do not add salt until the last minute, as it tends to harden them.

French beans

To prepare French beans (haricots verts), snap off each tip by hand and pull away together with any 'strings' from the edges.

To cook French beans deliciously: simmer first in chicken

stock or bouillon until tender but still crunchy (about 8 minutes), then drain and toss in another pan for 1 minute with olive oil and crushed garlic.

Beetroot

Beetroot should be cooked whole, complete with its skin, root and a little of the stalk, so that none of the juice escapes. Simply wash first, then simmer for $1\frac{1}{2}$ to 2 hours, until the skin slips off easily.

Cabbage

A piece of bread or a dash of lemon juice added to the cooking water will cut down the smell of boiling cabbage.

If you boil the water before adding the cabbage and cook it for only 10 minutes, it won't go soggy. Serve with salt, freshly ground black pepper and a knob of butter.

Alternatively, cook cabbage like this. Soften a small chopped onion in 2 tablespoons of oil, add a crushed clove of garlic if you like garlic, then add the washed and shredded leaves of a medium cabbage and a good pinch of caraway seeds. Toss the cabbage to coat the leaves with oil, then cover and cook gently (without adding any liquid) for 10 minutes. Serve crunchy.

Carrots

Improve the flavour of frozen or tinned carrots by sautéing them for a minute or two, just before serving, with 1 oz (25 g) of butter, a pinch of sugar and a squeeze of lemon juice. Season with salt and freshly ground black pepper, and a grating of fresh nutmeg.

French-style carrots

For 4 people: soften a crushed garlic clove in 2 oz (50 g) of butter for 2 minutes, then toss 1 lb (450 g) of lightly cooked carrots in the pan until glazed. Sprinkle with chopped fresh parsley, salt and black pepper to serve.

Cauliflower

A bay leaf added to the water counteracts the smell of boiling cauliflower.

Cauliflower au gratin

Divide cauliflower into florets, cook in boiling salted water until tender but still firm (about 4 minutes), arrange in an ovenproof dish, sprinkle with grated cheese and bread-crumbs, and grill for 3 minutes before serving.

Cauliflower leaves

Don't discard cauliflower leaves. Clean and chop them, boil until just tender but still firm, and serve with melted butter as a vegetable in their own right.

Or, use them to flavour stocks and soups.

Sautéed cauliflower

To preserve all the flavour of cauliflower – which is some-times lost in boiling – divide it into florets and sauté it in olive oil instead.

Celery

For extra crisp celery, stand the stalks in iced water for half an hour before serving.

Corn on the cob

To remove the silk threads quickly, wipe the cob from top to bottom with a clean damp towel or paper kitchen towel.

To remove the corn itself, use a shoehorn.

Cucumber

If cucumber gives you indigestion, slice it a few hours before it is to be eaten, sprinkle with salt and leave to drain. Discard liquid before serving or cooking.

Dressing salads

When making a salad from cooked ingredients, such as beans, or rice or potatoes, add the dressing while they are still warm so that they absorb all its flavour.

Garlic-flavoured salads

If you like only a mild flavour of garlic, rub the cut side of half a garlic clove around the salad bowl before putting the salad in it.

Leeks

To get the most flavour out of leeks, don't boil them, but braise them gently, chopped into 1-inch (3-cm) pieces in a tablespoon of butter in a heavy covered pan for 15 minutes.

Alternatively, steam them until tender but still firm, and toss while still warm in a vinaigrette dressing (page 101). Serve warm or cold.

Don't waste the green part of leeks: use them to flavour soups and stocks.

Lettuce

When preparing a salad, don't cut lettuce leaves with a knife, or they will go brown. Tear them instead.

Mange tout

Mange tout (young peapods, peas and all) should be served crunchy. Top and tail the pods, toss them in a tablespoon of butter in a heavy pan, add salt, and cook for one or two minutes over a medium heat.

Onions

To prevent tears when chopping onions, put them in the freezing compartment of the fridge for fifteen minutes first.

Also, leave the root on while you are chopping.

To chop an onion efficiently and quickly, first cut it in half and cut each half into thin slices, cut side down. Then chop the slices finely with a sharp knife, holding the tip with one hand and the handle with the other, and using the tip as a fixed pivot while moving the rest of the blade backwards and forwards in a semi-circle, chopping all the time.

When a recipe calls for a 'finely chopped' onion, it is quicker to grate it.

If you object to the strong smell and flavour of onions, combine them with celery. This will modify the taste, and make the onions more digestible.

Or, if you find the flavour of raw onion too powerful in salads, soak the slices in cold water for an hour before serving.

To remove the smell of onions from cutlery, plates and hands, rub with raw celery leaves.

French-style peas

For 4 people: put 1 lb (450 g) of freshly shelled peas into a heavy saucepan with 2 tablespoons of butter, 1 quartered fresh lettuce, 1 finely chopped onion, 1 dessertspoon of sugar and 1 teaspoon of salt. Add water to cover and simmer gently until the peas are just tender.

Peeling peppers

To peel peppers and aubergines, hold on a toasting fork over a gas burner for a few minutes until the skin is charred. It can then be easily removed.

Salad servers

Wooden servers are better than metal ones: metal ones tend to bruise the salad leaves.

Spinach

Improve the flavour of tinned or frozen spinach by adding, just before serving, a spoonful or two of single cream, a pinch of salt and some freshly grated nutmeg and black pepper.

Three-bean salad

Combine equal amounts of three different kinds of cooked pulses – haricot beans, red kidney beans, chick peas, soya beans, black beans, lentils, black-eyed peas – whatever you like. Season well and toss them in a generous helping of vinaigrette dressing (see below) so that they are well lubricated. (If they are freshly cooked, do this while they are still warm.) Leave to stand for the flavours to mingle, then serve garnished with chopped fresh parsley or tarragon.

Turnips

To get the full flavour of young turnips, peel them and cut into 1-inch (3-cm) cubes. Cook in boiling water for 3 minutes, then toss in butter for 5 minutes more. Serve with chopped fresh parsley or chives.

Vinaigrette dressing

Make a large quantity of vinaigrette to store in the fridge, to save time. Put 8 tablespoons of olive oil in a screw-top jar together with 2 tablespoons of white wine vinegar, a generous pinch of salt, plenty of freshly ground black pepper and ¼ teaspoon of dry mustard. Shake vigorously to blend all of the ingredients each time before using. Don't put garlic and fresh herbs in a dressing that you are going to store: chop them and add them fresh to each salad as you make it.

Bread and Cereals

Here are some hints about how to make better bread – and also different kinds of bread. There are recipes for making emergency bread or rolls without yeast; and, for a change, Scottish oatcakes, Mexican tortillas, American cornbread and Indian chapatis. They are all astonishingly simple and different, and very good to eat.

There are also some suggestions about alternative cereals – not the kind that come in packets for breakfast, but the different grains that can be ground into flour. If you're bored with the choice between potatoes or rice or packet pasta when cooking a main meal, then take a look at the recipes that follow. Lend a Middle Eastern, a northern Italian, an Indian flavour to a meal with bulgur, polenta or dhal; and if you want to pretend you're in Naples, try making your own pasta. None of these dishes is difficult: all are made with plain, basic ingredients, and any will add a refreshing new dimension to your cooking.

Bread

To speed up breadmaking, warm your flour in a slow oven for a few minutes before mixing the dough.

The more salt you add to your dough, the longer it will take to prove.

If you haven't got an airing cupboard for your dough to prove in, wrap the mixing bowl securely in a polythene bag (with a few drops of oil in it) and stand it in a basin of warm water until the dough has doubled in size.

For a soft surface texture on home-made bread, brush the loaf with milk and then sprinkle with flour, just before baking.

For a crisp, light crust, brush with oil.

For a crunchy crust, brush with salty water when half-baked, then sprinkle with cracked wheat, sunflower seeds, crushed cornflakes or oatmeal.

Breadcrumbs

The 'golden' breadcrumbs you can buy in packets are often powdery and tasteless. Make your own superior breadcrumbs by grating stale bread and frying the crumbs in butter or dripping until golden and crunchy. Drain on kitchen towels, cool and store in an airtight container for up to a month.

Breadcrumb substitute

Crushed cornflakes can be used instead of breadcrumbs for

coating food to be deep fried, in treacle tarts, and to make a crunchy topping for puddings.

Bulgur (*Middle East*)

Make your own bulgur by cooking whole wheat grains in twice their volume of water for 45 minutes, or until just tender. Drain, reserving any remaining liquid for soup-making, and spread the grains out on baking trays. Dry out in the oven at gas mark $\frac{1}{2}$, 250°F, 130°C, then cool, grind coarsely and store in airtight containers. Use like rice, to accompany meat and poultry, and in salads: it has a delicious nutty flavour.

Chapati (*India*)

To make 4 chapati, combine 8 oz (225 g) of wholemeal flour with 1 teaspoon of salt on a pastry board. Sprinkle a little cold water into a well in the centre and work in gradually until about $\frac{3}{8}$ pint (210 ml) has been absorbed and the dough is elastic. Knead energetically for 5 minutes, then cover with a damp cloth and leave for half an hour. Knead again lightly, then form into small balls and roll out into paper-thin rounds about 8 inches (20 cm) across. Cook for a minute or so on each side on a lightly greased medium-hot griddle or in a heavy frying pan, until the chapati begins to brown and puff up. Serve hot, with curry.

Cornbread (*United States*)

This is the American equivalent of Yorkshire pudding. Combine 6 oz (175 g) of cornmeal, 4 oz (125 g) of plain flour, 3 oz (75 g) of sugar, 3 teaspoons of baking powder and 1 teaspoon of salt, then add $\frac{1}{2}$ pint (275 ml) of milk, 1 beaten egg and 2 tablespoons of melted butter. Pour into a shallow buttered tin, about 8 inches (20 cm) square, and bake at gas mark 7, 425°F, 220°C, for 20 minutes until well risen and golden. Serve hot.

Dhal (*India*)

Wash 4 oz (125 g) of red lentils – they don't need soaking – and simmer them in ½ pint (275 ml) of water for 1 hour. Meanwhile, cook a crushed clove of garlic and a finely chopped onion in dripping or oil. Stir these into the lentils when they are tender, together with a dessertspoon of garam masala. Serve hot with curry.

Dried yeast

One level tablespoon or ½ oz (15 g) of dried yeast is equivalent to 1 oz (25 g) of fresh yeast.

Lasagne (*Southern Italy*)

When preparing a large quantity of lasagne, cook just a few pieces at a time in a huge pan of rapidly boiling, salted water with a few drops of oil added. When they are cooked, take them out with a fish slice and put in a large bowl of cold water so that the pieces don't stick together.

Oatcakes (*Scotland*)

To make 3 oatcakes (12 quarters): mix 8 oz (225 g) of medium oatmeal with 3 oz (75 g) of plain flour and ½ teaspoon each of salt and bicarbonate of soda. Melt 2 oz (50 g) of dripping, pour this into a well in the centre and mix to a moist dough with about 8 tablespoons of hot water. Knead lightly on a floured board and divide into three, roll out into 8-inch (20-cm) rounds and cook on a hot greased griddle for 7 minutes on one side, until the edges begin to curl. Toast the top under a slow grill, and cool before serving with cheese.

Home-made pasta (*Italy*)

To make pasta for 6 people: combine 1 lb (450 g) of sifted plain flour with 1 teaspoon of salt in a large bowl. Crack

2 eggs into a well in the centre, add 2 teaspoons of olive oil, and start to work the flour into the liquids with a fork. When half the flour is incorporated, work in the rest by hand; then knead the dough on a floured board for 10 minutes until it is smooth and elastic.

Divide into two and roll each piece out into a thin strip, then fold into three and roll out again. Repeat this process three or four times until the rolled-out paste is so thin that you can see through it. Hang over chairbacks (on clean tea towels) for 30 minutes at least, then cut into the shapes you want. (For tagliatelle, roll up the paste and cut with a sharp knife into strips about ½ inch [1 cm] wide.)

To cook fresh pasta: drop into a huge pan of rapidly boiling salted water with a dash of olive oil added. Cook for about 5 minutes only, or until it rises to the surface. Drain and serve very hot with butter, salt, freshly ground black pepper and freshly grated Parmesan, or with fresh tomato sauce (page 116).

When pasta is just cooked, add a tablespoon of cold water to the pan before draining. This will help to stop it sticking together.

To separate strands of spaghetti after it is cooked, toss it in a clean pan with a little olive oil (2 tablespoons for every 1 lb [450 g] of spaghetti).

Or, pour boiling water over it.

Polenta (*Northern Italy*)

For 4 people: bring a huge panful of salted water to the boil, then reduce heat so that it is just simmering. Pour into it slowly 1 lb (450 g) of coarsely ground cornmeal, and stir all the time with a wooden spoon, to avoid lumps. Simmer, stirring frequently, for 20 minutes, until the polenta is so thick that it comes away from the sides of the pan. Then pour it out on to a hot flat dish and serve hot, with knobs of butter, to accompany spicy grilled sausages or other meat. *Or*, cool, slice and fry.

Home-made popcorn

There is a world of difference between this and what you get at the cinema. Put about 1 tablespoon of oil together with a tablespoon of popping corn into a heavy pan with a tightly fitting lid. Heat steadily, covered, for about 5 minutes, until the popping sounds subside (don't peep until they do). Meanwhile melt a dollop of butter in another pan, and pour this over the popped corn in a large bowl with salt to taste. (Some people prefer sugar.)

NB If popping corn is not stored in an airtight container it may dry out and refuse to pop. If this happens to yours, simply soak the corn in warm water for a few minutes, then drain thoroughly before popping.

Authentic porridge (Scotland)

For 4 people: bring 2 pints (1 litre) of water to the boil, then sprinkle into it 5 oz (150 g) of medium oatmeal. Whisk until it comes back to the boil, then reduce heat, cover and simmer for 10 minutes. Stir in 2 teaspoons of salt and cook for 15 minutes more. Serve with cream or milk, and soft brown sugar.

To keep rice hot

If you need to keep cooked rice hot, stand the container over a pan of simmering water and cover it with a clean tea towel. The cloth will absorb steam from the rice – rather than allowing it to condense, as a metal lid would – and will keep it dry.

Soda bread

Combine 1 lb (450 g) of wholemeal or plain flour with 2 teaspoons each of salt and bicarbonate of soda. Whisk together ¼ pint each of sour cream or natural yoghurt and water (or

½ pint [275 ml] of milk with 4 teaspoons of cream of tartar), and stir into the flour mixture. Knead lightly, shape into a round loaf, mark into triangles and bake at gas mark 7, 425°F, 220°C for 30 minutes. Cool and eat the same day.

Tortillas (Mexico)

To make 12 tortillas: combine 10 oz (275 g) of finely ground cornmeal with 1 teaspoon of salt, then stir in ½ pint (275 ml) of boiling water. Knead the dough lightly, form into 12 balls, and roll out into thin rounds. Cook on a lightly greased griddle or in a cast-iron frying pan until browning on both sides. Serve hot.

Wheatmeal bread

If you find wholemeal bread too heavy, use a combination of half wholemeal flour and half plain flour to make a 'wheatmeal' loaf.

Yeastless loaf

Sift 1 lb (450 g) of self-raising flour with 1 level teaspoon of salt, then stir in ½ pint (275 ml) of milk and mix to a rough dough. Knead lightly on a floured surface, form into a round, 1 inch (3 cm) thick, and bake on a floured baking sheet at gas mark 5, 375°F, 190°C for 30 minutes or until crisp and firm. Eat soon.

Yeastless rolls

Pour ¼ pint (150 ml) of water into a well in the centre of 8 oz (225 g) self-raising flour and 1 teaspoon of salt. Work into a soft dough with a fork, then knead for a minute or two on a floured surface. Shape into 8 rolls, and bake on a greased baking sheet at gas mark 7, 425°F, 220°C for 20 minutes. Eat at once.

Sauces and Seasonings

Here are some ideas for making sauce-making simpler, as well as some quick and totally unmysterious recipes. I recommend them not just because it's a great deal more satisfying to eat your own fresh lemon sauce, or fresh tomato sauce, or fresh parsley butter or mayonnaise, and not just because they're cheaper, but because they really do taste twice as good as the ones that come in bottles and tins.

The golden rules in sauce-making are delicacy and freshness. Remember that sauces and flavourings are meant to complement and enhance a dish, not to disguise it. Too little is better than too much. Use seasonings sparingly, tasting as you go along: people can always add more at the table if they wish. Always use freshly ground black pepper, freshly grated nutmeg and Parmesan: they are no more expensive than the ready-grated versions, but their flavours are infinitely richer. If you have a grinder, or a pestle and mortar and lots of energy, grind your own spices for making curry or chilli: it's worth it for the smell alone, but there's even more pleasure to be had in the eating.

Use fresh herbs whenever you can: they add a far subtler, sweeter flavour. But if you have to use dried herbs, store them in a cool dark place and don't keep them for more than a month or two, or they will develop a bitter, stale taste. Remember in any case that dried herbs have a more potent flavour than fresh ones, and should be used only in tiny quantities.

Avgolemono (*Greek lemon sauce*)

Beat 2 eggs in a saucepan, add 1 tablespoon of cornflour, the juice of 1 lemon, and 1 pint (575 ml) of boiling chicken stock. Heat, whisking all the time, until the sauce is thick and frothy. Serve with chicken, fish or meatballs.

Bacon trimmings

Buy bacon trimmings from the butcher to use for flavouring soups and stews.

Barbecue sauce

Soften 1 finely chopped onion in butter, stir in 1 teaspoon of tomato purée and cook for 3 minutes. Then add a mixture of 2 tablespoons each of vinegar, brown sugar and Worcester sauce, 2 teaspoons of dry mustard and ¼ pint (150 ml) of water. Simmer for 10 minutes before serving.

Home-made beef stock

Roast 3 lb (1·5 kg) of beef marrow bones, cut into pieces, together with 2 chopped onions, 2 chopped carrots and 2 chopped celery stalks, for 45 minutes. Transfer to a large saucepan, cover with 5 pints (3 litres) of cold water, add a little dried thyme, parsley, salt and a few black peppercorns. Bring to the boil, skim, and simmer for 4 hours. Strain, cool and remove fat before use.

Beurre manié

This is simply a mixture of butter and flour which can be used for thickening sauces quickly. Mix 3 oz (75 g) of butter together with 2 oz (50 g) of flour using a fork, until they form a smooth paste. Add a few small knobs of this to the sauce while it is simmering. Do not stir it in, but simply tip the pan to allow the *beurre manié* to spread. When the sauce thickens – after a few seconds – serve at once.

If you make larger quantities of *beurre manié* you can store it in the fridge in a screw-top jar and use as required.

Home-made bouquet garni

Wrap sprigs of parsley and thyme, a bay leaf and a strip of orange peel in a curl of leek (instead of muslin). Use for adding flavour to simmering stews. Remember to remove before serving.

Bread sauce

You don't need to make breadcrumbs for a bread sauce. First, put a whole peeled onion into 1 pint (575 ml) of milk with a bay leaf, bring to the boil, then remove from the heat, cover and leave to infuse for 30 minutes. Take out and discard the onion and bay leaf, add 3 thick slices of bread without crusts and leave to soak for 10 minutes. Beat to a purée with a wooden spoon, then cook gently until the sauce is thick, adding $\frac{1}{2}$ oz (15 g) of butter, 1 tablespoon of cream and salt and pepper to taste.

Brown stock

When making stock from meat bones, brown them first under a hot grill and the stock will have a deep rich colour.

Cheese sauce

Make a cheese sauce more interesting by adding a sprinkling of dry mustard, a pinch of cayenne pepper and a dash of lemon juice.

Cooking with cider

When cooking with cider, do not use an iron or tin pan as it will turn the cider black. Use an enamelled or porcelain-lined pan instead.

To clarify stock

If your home-made stock is cloudy, add some empty eggshells to it for 10 minutes while it is simmering.

Seasoning cold dishes

When serving a cooked savoury dish cold, always check the seasoning at the last minute. You may need to add more, as flavours tend to diminish as food cools.

Custard

A teaspoonful of cornflour added to real egg custard will prevent it curdling.

Dried herbs

The flavour of dried herbs is powerful and they should be used sparingly: one teaspoon of dried herbs is equivalent to two teaspoons of fresh ones.

Filming

If you make a white sauce, such as a cheese sauce or béchamel, in advance, put a few dots of butter on top while it is still hot to prevent a skin forming.

Garlic

If you haven't got a garlic press, crush a clove of garlic together with a pinch of salt under the blade of a knife. The salt brings out the garlic juices and forms a kind of paste.

Garlic should be cooked very gently at first – just softened until transparent. Do not allow it to brown, or it will develop a powerful bitter flavour.

Gravy

To make brown gravy without using gravy browning, place a tablespoon of flour in a small bowl in the oven alongside the meat while it is cooking. When the meat is ready the flour will be browned.

Horseradish sauce

Grate 2 tablespoons of fresh horseradish and combine with 2 teaspoons each of lemon juice and sugar, a pinch of dry mustard and a small carton of whipped double cream. Serve with beef or fish.

Mace

If you need mace for a recipe and can't get it, use nutmeg instead, but use more of it. It comes from the same plant as mace and has a similar, but milder, flavour.

Mayonnaise

If you make mayonnaise a day or two before it is to be used, add a couple of teaspoons of boiling water to the mixture after it is blended. This prevents it separating or turning oily. Store in a cool place.

Blender mayonnaise

This is infallible, since, as Julia Child says, 'No culinary skill whatsoever enters into its preparation.'

Blend a whole egg with $\frac{1}{2}$ teaspoon salt and $\frac{1}{4}$ teaspoon dry mustard for 30 seconds, then add 1 tablespoon of lemon juice or wine vinegar and blend for 10 seconds more. Now add a scant $\frac{1}{2}$ pint (275 ml) of olive oil very gradually, drop by drop at first, through the lid, blending all the time. (The mayonnaise won't start to thicken until half of the oil has been added.) When it is all blended, transfer to a screw-top jar and store in the fridge for up to a week.

Mint sauce

Wine vinegar gives a more subtle flavour than malt vinegar, and is less likely to overwhelm the taste of the lamb. Use 1 tablespoon of wine vinegar for every 3 tablespoons of chopped fresh mint, together with 3 tablespoons of water.

Mushroom flavour

Keep a jar of mushroom ketchup for adding a subtle flavour to gravies and sauces.

Mustard

Always use cold water to mix mustard; and mix it at least ten minutes before serving, to allow the flavour to develop.

Onion stems

If you grow your own onions or spring onions, you can use the stems like chives for flavouring soups and stews.

Parsley

Even when parsley is used in cooking a dish, rather than garnishing it, it should not usually be added until about five minutes before the end of the cooking time. If cooked for a long time it tends to develop a bitter flavour.

Parsley butter

Chop three tablespoons of fresh parsley very finely. Rinse out a mixing bowl with hot water, and, using a fork, work the parsley together with 4 oz (125 g) of butter and a few drops of lemon juice. Chill until firm and serve with hot vegetables or fish.

Reheating

When reheating a white sauce, don't put the pan directly over the heat in case it burns. Instead, stand it in another pan of simmering water.

A white sauce made with cornflour rather than flour will reheat more smoothly. Use ½ oz (15 g) of cornflour in place of 1 oz (25 g) of flour.

Saffron

To get the full flavour and colour from saffron in the form of pistils, rather than powder, crush about six pistils and add to two tablespoons of hot stock or water. Leave to soak until the liquid turns bright orange, then strain and add to other ingredients.

Salt

When you double the ingredients in a recipe, you won't need twice as much salt, but only one-and-a-half times as much.

Tarragon

If you are using dried tarragon, soak it in warm water for a few minutes first to bring out the flavour.

Home-made tartare sauce

Combine ¼ pint (150 ml) of mayonnaise (page 114) with 1 tablespoon of lemon juice, 2 teaspoons each of chopped gherkins, chopped capers and chopped parsley, and 1 teaspoon of chopped chives. Leave to stand for at least 1 hour.

Fresh tomato sauce

Heat 1 tablespoon of olive oil in a heavy pan, cook a crushed clove of garlic and 1 chopped onion in it gently until transparent, then add 1 chopped carrot, 1 lb (450 g) of peeled and chopped tomatoes (tinned Italian ones are just as good as fresh), 1 tablespoon of tomato purée, some chopped fresh herbs such as parsley, marjoram and basil, a pinch of salt, a pinch of sugar and some freshly ground black pepper. Simmer for about half an hour, until the tomatoes are reduced to a pulp. Serve with pasta, meatballs, etc.

Vanilla pods

Vanilla pods can be used over and over again. After cooking them in a sweet dish, simply fish out, dry and store in an airtight container.

White sauce

If you heat the milk before making a white sauce you will find that it blends in more smoothly and quickly.

Ten-minute Puddings

If you're cooking a meal in a hurry after racing around all day, you may think everyone will understand if you don't find time to make a pudding, or whip up something out of a packet, or hopefully arrange a pretty bowl of fruit. But in fact, of course, they won't. A pudding makes all the difference. There is nothing more certain to win friends and influence people, impress dinner party guests, soothe fractious children, seduce a new lover or an old husband, than a pudding.

So if your problem is lack of time, or lack of inspiration,

here are some suggestions. None takes more than ten minutes to prepare – several take less – and although some of the puddings need to chill before serving, you'll usually find that if you make them before you start preparing the rest of the meal, they'll be ready when you're ready to eat them.

Several of the recipes can be made with the help of that fruitbowl: so do try always to have lemons or oranges or apples in store. Eggs are essential. Thankfully, you don't need to make pastry. (A biscuit-crumb crust is much quicker.) Some of the recipes are traditional British ones – syllabub and junket, hasty pudding and egg custard – but then there are one or two Continental ideas too, like sweet soufflé omelette, chocolate mousse, and the unforgettable, intoxicating zabaglione. All, in next to no time, make tempting, original and deeply satisfying desserts.

Baked apples

Wash even-sized cooking apples and remove cores using a potato peeler. Run a sharp knife round the middle of each apple, just cutting through the skin (to allow the skin to shrink during baking), then stand in a baking tin and put a spoonful of brown sugar and raisins, a sprinkling of cinnamon and a knob of butter into each core. Pour a little water into the tin, just to cover the bottom, and bake at gas mark 4, 350°F, 180°C for 30 minutes. Serve with syrup from the tin and cream.

Banana boats

For 4 people: make a chocolate sauce with 1 oz (25 g) each of margarine, cocoa and sugar with 1 tablespoon of golden syrup, 2 tablespoons of water and $\frac{1}{2}$ teaspoon vanilla essence. Heat all together gently until the cocoa has dissolved. (Do not boil or the shine will disappear.) Slice 4 bananas lengthwise, sandwich together with vanilla ice cream, pour over the chocolate sauce, sprinkle with toasted nuts and decorate with wafer 'sails'.

Banana nut cream

For 4 people: whip together lightly a small carton each of single and double cream. Add this to 4 mashed ripe bananas, 1 tablespoon of lemon juice, 2 level tablespoons of sugar and 2 heaped tablespoons of chopped nuts. Serve chilled in individual dishes.

Blackcurrant brûlée

Cook 8 oz (225 g) of blackcurrants with 3 oz (75 g) of soft brown sugar and ¼ pint (150 ml) water for 5 minutes. Blend 1½ tablespoons of arrowroot into a tablespoon of water, stir this into the fruit mixture and cook for 2 minutes more. Transfer to an ovenproof serving dish, cool, spread a small carton of sour cream and a sprinkling of soft brown sugar over the top, and place under a hot grill for 1 minute before serving, so that the cream and sugar are brown and bubbly.

Buckwheat pancakes

To make 10–12 pancakes, beat together 2 eggs, 2 tablespoons of olive oil, 3 tablespoons of honey and 1 pint (575 ml) of buttermilk. Combine 9 oz (250 g) of buckwheat flour, 3 oz (75 g) of wholemeal flour, 1½ teaspoons of baking powder and ½ teaspoon of salt, add the liquid ingredients and blend in a liquidizer. Cook on a hot, lightly greased griddle or in a heavy frying pan until golden on both sides. Serve hot with lots of butter and maple syrup.

Butterscotch ice cream

For 4 people: heat 2 oz (50 g) of butter with 4 oz (125 g) of brown sugar and 4 oz (125 g) of golden syrup. Cook gently for 5 minutes, then remove from heat and stir in 3 tablespoons of milk or single cream. Serve hot or cold with vanilla ice cream.

Caramel ice cream

For 4 people: boil 3 oz (75 g) of sugar with 3 tablespoons of water until the caramel is golden, then blend in 3 more table-spoons of water. Cool and serve with vanilla ice cream.

Instant cheesecake

Melt 2 oz (50 g) of butter with a dessertspoon of syrup and stir in 10 crushed digestive biscuits. Mix thoroughly and press into an 8-inch (20-cm) flan case. Whisk together 6 oz (175 g) of cream cheese, a small tin of condensed milk, and the juice and grated rind of 1 large lemon. Tip into the flan case and chill for several hours. Decorate if you like with halved grapes.

Chocolate mousse

For 4 people: melt 4 oz (125 g) of plain chocolate (*not* cooking chocolate) in a small basin over a pan of simmering water. Remove from heat, add $\frac{1}{2}$ oz (15 g) of unsalted butter, then beat in 3 egg yolks and the grated rind of 1 orange. Whisk 3 egg whites until stiff, fold into chocolate mixture and turn into separate dishes to chill. Serve with whipped cream.

Egg custard

For 4 people: beat 4 egg yolks with $\frac{1}{2}$ pint (275 ml) of milk and strain into a saucepan through a fine sieve. Add 1 level tablespoon of sugar and heat for 10 minutes until thickened. Beat in a few drops of vanilla essence and serve hot or cold with fresh fruit.

Fruit fool

For 4 people: wash and prepare $1\frac{1}{2}$ lb (675 g) of soft fruit (apples, apricots, blackberries, blackcurrants, damsons, gooseberries, plums or rhubarb), then cook gently in 2 tablespoons of water until soft. Stir in 4 oz (125 g) of sugar, cool, and fold in a small carton of lightly whipped double cream. Serve chilled.

Hasty pudding

For 4 people: melt 1 oz (25 g) of butter in a saucepan and stir in 1 heaped tablespoon of flour or cornflour. When blended add ¾ pint (425 ml) of warm milk, stirring all the time until smooth and thick. Add a pinch of mace or nutmeg and simmer for 2 minutes. Then pour into a well-buttered ovenproof dish, dot with small lumps of butter, cover with 2 tablespoons of soft brown sugar and a teaspoon of nutmeg or cinnamon. Put under a hot grill for 3 minutes until browned. Serve hot or cold.

'Ice cream' pudding

For 6 people: heat 1 pint (575 ml) of milk with 2 oz (50 g) of butter. Meanwhile mix 2 rounded tablespoons of cornflour with 2 egg yolks and a tablespoon of cold milk in a bowl. Pour in the hot milk, then return to the pan and boil, stirring, for 1 minute. Transfer to an ovenproof dish. Whisk 2 egg whites with 2 rounded tablespoons of caster sugar until very stiff, pile over the custard and brown in a hot oven (gas mark 7, 425°F, 220°C) for 10 minutes.

Jelly cream

For 4 people: make up a jelly with ¾ pint (425 ml) of water instead of a full pint. When it is beginning to set, whisk in a small carton of single cream or plain yoghurt, or a small tin of evaporated milk.

Junket

Warm 1 pint (575 ml) of milk to blood heat, add 1 tablespoon of honey or sugar, a few drops of vanilla essence or rum or other flavouring and 1 teaspoon of rennet, and pour into a bowl to cool and set. Serve with fresh fruit and cream.

Lemon flan

Crush 4 oz (125 g) of digestive biscuits in a mixing bowl with the end of a rolling pin. Melt 2 oz (50 g) of butter in a saucepan, add the crumbs and 1 tablespoon of sugar. Press into an 8-inch (20-cm) pie dish and bake at gas mark 2, 300°F, 150°C for 5 minutes. Meanwhile mix together a small carton of double cream, a small tin of evaporated milk, and the grated rind and the juice of 2 lemons. Pour into the flan case and chill until firm.

Lemon soufflé omelette

For 2 people: beat 3 egg yolks with 2 dessertspoons of caster sugar and the juice and grated rind of 1 lemon. Whisk 3 egg whites until stiff, fold into the yolks and cook for about 1 minute in foaming butter in an omelette pan until the bottom is set. Brown under a hot grill and serve at once.

Sweet omelette

For 4 people: separate 5 eggs, beat the yolks with 1 level tablespoon of sugar and 2 tablespoons of single cream or top-of-the-milk. Whisk the whites until very stiff and fold into the yolks. Melt a knob of butter in an omelette pan, and when it is foaming pour in the egg mixture. Cook for 1 minute, until the bottom is set, then place under a hot grill to cook the top. Add 4 tablespoons of heated jam or fruit purée, fold over, dust with icing sugar and serve at once.

Grilled oranges

For 4 people: peel 4 oranges, divide into segments and arrange in a shallow ovenproof dish. Pour a small carton of double cream over them, sprinkle with soft brown sugar and place under a hot grill for 5 minutes, until sugar is melted and bubbling. Serve hot or cold.

Orange cream

For 4 people: mix the grated rind of 1 large orange, the juice of 2 large oranges, a large carton of sour cream (or double cream with a tablespoon of lemon juice), and 1 tablespoon of caster sugar. Pour into individual glasses and serve chilled, with sponge fingers for dipping.

Instant Swiss roll

For 3 people: beat 2 eggs, add 3 dessertspoons of sugar, 2 tablespoons of plain flour and 1 dessertspoon of baking powder. Mix well and spread thinly in a lightly buttered shallow baking tin, 9½ by 8 inches (24 by 20 cm). Bake at gas mark 7, 425°F, 220°C for 10 minutes, then spread with a thin layer of jam, roll up and serve with cream or egg custard (page 120).

Syllabub

For 4 people: whip a large carton of double cream. In a separate bowl, whisk 2 egg whites until stiff, then fold into them 4 level tablespoons of caster sugar, the juice of half a lemon, a glass of sweet white wine or sherry, and the cream. Pour into individual glasses and chill for several hours. Serve with sponge fingers.

Zabaglione

For 2 people: beat 3 egg yolks with 1 tablespoon of caster sugar and 3 tablespoons of Marsala in a basin over a pan of simmering water until thick and creamy. Serve at once with sponge fingers.

Better Baking

Home-made cakes and pastries are a luxury these days, because most cooks assume that they take lots of time, and are thankful enough to get the right number of meals on the table, without trying to fit baking into their busy days as well. And because we're losing the habit of home-baking, it's becoming more mysterious: there are so many things that can go wrong – hollow cakes, runny icing, soggy pastry. So here are some hints which are designed to speed up baking and to de-mystify it. There are also recipes for 'all-in-one' instant cakes, fool-proof meringues, quick flaky pastry – and suggestions about how to avoid making pastry at all.

Biscuits

To save cutting out biscuits individually with rings, roll the dough into a long sausage and slice it thinly.

Brown sugar

If your brown sugar has gone hard and you haven't time to soften it, grate as much as you need with a grater.

Cold butter

If you need to cream butter that has been in the refrigerator, grate it first into a warmed bowl.

Cake-making

It saves bothering with scales if you remember that 1 oz (25 g) of flour is a heaped tablespoon, and 1 oz (25 g) of white sugar is a level tablespoon.

Cake tins

Before using cake tins for the first time, grease them thoroughly and place in the oven at gas mark 2, 300°F, 150°C, for 15 minutes to season them.

Shallow tins can prevent a sponge sandwich rising. Sandwich tins should be at least 1½ inches (4 cm) deep.

To ensure an even distribution of heat when baking cakes, always leave a space between cake tins in the oven, and a space between the tins and the oven walls.

To ensure that the two halves of a sponge sandwich rise

evenly and cook at the same rate, place them both on the same oven shelf.

Fruit cakes

Before putting a rich fruit cake in the oven, hollow out the centre so that it will have a nice flat top when cooked.

If a fruit cake has gone dry, or if you want to make a rich fruit cake richer while you are storing it, make holes in the top with a skewer or knitting needle and pour in a teaspoon or two of brandy.

All-in-one fruit cake

Sift 8 oz (225 g) of self-raising flour with 1 teaspoon of mixed spice, then add 4 oz (125 g) each of caster sugar and quick-creaming margarine, 6 oz (175 g) of mixed dried fruit, 2 oz (50 g) of washed and halved glacé cherries, 2 eggs and 2 tablespoons of milk, mix well and beat with a wooden spoon for 1 minute. Bake in a lined 6-inch (15-cm) tin at gas mark 3, 325°F, 170°C for 1½ to 2 hours. Cool before turning out.

Icing cakes

Use fancily shaped biscuit cutters to mark out patterns to ice on a cake.

Or, mark out your own design with pin pricks. (Sterilize the pin first in a match flame.)

If you lose your plain icing cone, use the top of the salt cellar instead.

When placing paper patterns on an iced cake to serve as a guide for decorating it, dip them in water first so that they won't stick to the icing.

If a freshly baked cake is too crumbly to ice, put it in the freezer for a few minutes until it is firm.

To save time when icing cupcakes, instead of spreading

icing on them individually with a palette knife, simply dip them in the icing one by one.

Don't waste leftover royal icing. Use it to pipe individual flowers, etc., on greaseproof paper or foil, then dry them and store in an airtight container to be used later.

Use the 'chisel' blade of a grater to make chocolate curls from a bar of plain chocolate, to decorate chocolate cakes.

Party cakes

Make novel cakes for children's parties in ice-cream wafers (with flat bottoms). Half-fill them with a favourite cake mix and bake as you would normally. Serve topped with ice-cream.

Serving cakes

To prevent a cake sticking to a serving plate, dust the plate with icing sugar first.

Use dental floss or heavy nylon thread to cut particularly fluffy cakes – like devil's food cake – cleanly.

All-in-one sponge cake

Sift 4 oz (125 g) of self-raising flour together with 1 teaspoon of baking powder, then add 4 oz (125 g) each of quick-creaming margarine and caster sugar, 2 eggs and 2 drops of vanilla essence. Whisk thoroughly, divide between two 7-inch (18-cm) greased and lined sandwich tins and bake in the centre of the oven at gas mark 3, 325°F, 170°C, for 30 minutes. Remove, cool and sandwich together with jam and cream.

Valentine's cake

To make a heart-shaped cake, bake a square one and a round one whose diameter is the same as the sides of the square.

Cut the round one in half, place it along two adjacent sides of the square, and ice.

Caramel

Dissolve granulated sugar in water (1 oz [25 g] of sugar for every tablespoon of water) and boil over a steady heat without stirring until golden brown.

Chantilly cream

Whisk a small carton of double cream. In a separate bowl whisk 1 egg white until stiff, then fold in the cream together with 1 tablespoon of caster sugar and a drop of vanilla essence. Serve chilled.

Eggs

You can tell whether an egg is cooked or not by spinning it. A cooked egg, because it is solid and its weight evenly distributed, will carry on spinning; but a raw egg will turn once and stop.

To separate eggs

The professional chef's way of separating an egg is to crack it into a cup, then tip it into the palm of one hand and allow the white to slip through the fingers.

Egg whites

The most efficient way to beat the white of just one egg is on a flat plate, using a knife. Add a pinch of salt to the white first.

If egg whites are at room temperature, the whites expand more when whipped. If you store your eggs in the refrigerator, take them out at least half an hour before you want to whip the whites.

Whisked egg whites will remain stiff for up to half an hour if covered and kept airtight. Either turn the mixing bowl upside down over a plate, or cover it tightly with silver foil.

Meringues

To make 12 individual meringues, whisk 2 egg whites until they are so stiff that you can turn the bowl upside down without them falling out. Beat in 4 oz (125 g) of caster sugar very gradually, a dessertspoonful at a time, so that the mixture remains very stiff. Place spoonfuls on oiled baking sheets and bake for up to 2 hours at gas mark ¼, 225°F, 110°C, until thoroughly dry and crisp. Remove from baking sheets carefully using a hot wet palette knife. Cool and store in an airtight container.

Pancakes

A dash of beer or soda water added to the batter for pancakes or fritters will make them extra light.

Make pancake batter in a jug so that you can easily pour it as required into the frying pan.

Extra pancakes can be stored, wrapped in polythene, in the fridge for several days. If you find that they stick together when you want to use them, heat them gently in a warm oven for a minute or two.

Pastry

Make up a large quantity of pastry mix – 2 lb (1 kg) of plain flour to 1 lb (500 g) of half-lard-and-half-margarine. Rub together until breadcrumb-like and store in a catering-size margarine container. It will keep in the refrigerator for at least two weeks, and with it you can make instant pastry by simply adding a little salt and cold water, or instant crumble topping by adding a little demerara sugar.

Alternative pastry

If you hate the sticky mess of rubbing fat into flour by hand, try the American method of chopping the fat and flour finely together with a knife – or even two knives, one in each hand.

Or, cream the fat together with a little water and just some of the flour (2 tablespoons of water and 4 tablespoons of flour to 8 oz [225 g] fat) using a fork, and then stir in the remaining flour.

Baking blind

Instead of using rice or dried peas for baking blind, place a second, smaller baking tin inside a pastry case for the first fifteen minutes of the cooking time.

Small pastry cases, for baby quiches, etc., can be baked blind on an upturned patty tin.

Quick flaky pastry

Put a packet of margarine in the freezing compartment of the fridge for half an hour. Sift together 8 oz (225 g) of plain flour and a pinch of salt, then grate 6 oz (175 g) of the margarine into the flour. Mix evenly, using a palette knife, then add a little cold water to make a dough. Put in the fridge for half an hour before rolling out.

Pastry substitutes

If you haven't time or the right ingredients to put a pastry crust on top of a pie, or if you're simply bored with pastry, try one of these toppings instead:

COBBLER

Make a scone dough by mixing a pinch of salt and 3 teaspoons of baking powder with 12 oz (350 g) of plain flour and then rubbing in 3 oz (75 g) of butter or margarine. Add water, milk, sour or single cream to make a smooth dough, knead lightly, roll out to ½ inch (2 cm) thick and cut into rounds. Arrange on top of pre-cooked filling, brush with milk or beaten egg and bake at gas mark 7, 425°F, 220°C for 10 minutes until risen and golden.

CRUMBLE

Add a pinch of salt to 5 oz (150 g) of plain flour and rub in 3 oz (75 g) of butter or margarine. For a sweet crumble, stir in 1 tablespoon of brown sugar; for a savoury crumble, add 1 tablespoon of grated cheese or chopped nuts. Spoon over pre-cooked filling, dot with butter and bake at gas mark 6, 400°F, 200°C, for 10 minutes until crisp and browning.

GOUGÈRE

Bring 2 oz (50 g) of butter and ½ pint (275 ml) of water (or milk, boiled, cooled and strained) to the boil, add 1 teaspoon of salt and a little freshly ground black pepper, then pour in 5 oz (150 g) of plain flour all at once. Stir to make a thick paste which comes away from the sides of the pan. Remove from the heat, stir in 3 eggs, one at a time, and then 3 oz (75 g) grated cheese. Spread or pipe on top of savoury filling, brush with milk, and bake at gas mark 5, 375°F, 190°C, for 45 minutes. (Do not peep at it in the meantime, or the gougère may collapse.)

Pie funnel

If you haven't got a pie funnel, stick a piece of macaroni into the centre of a pie crust while cooking to allow the juices to bubble up through it.

Scones

Use sour milk or yoghurt instead of milk to make scones, and they will be lighter.

Steaming puddings

Put a marble in the pan when steaming puddings: it will rattle and warn you if the pan boils dry.

Stand the pudding basin on an upturned saucer or two crossed meat skewers to raise it off the bottom of the saucepan.

Decorating tarts

Use pinking shears to cut strips of pastry for decorating tarts.

Measuring treacle

If you put a tin of treacle in a warm oven for a few minutes before you use it, the treacle will be runnier and easier to measure.

Fruit and Preserves

Preserving, like baking, is an art which the spare-time cook tends to regard with awe. But the hints and recipes in this chapter are chosen to show how simply you can treat yourself to blackberry wine or pickled cabbage, lemon curd or apple butter, rhubarb chutney or raspberry jam. There's an extra-speedy way of pickling onions, and a jam that doesn't need cooking at all. There are hints to solve classic jam-related problems such as sinking fruit, peeling labels, scum, mould and not setting. And others on more efficient ways of peeling, drying, stewing, puréeing and serving different kinds of fruit.

Apples

If you pour boiling water over apples or pears and let them steep in it for a minute you will find them much easier to peel.

Apple butter

Simmer 2 lb (1 kg) of chopped apples in ¾ pint (425 ml) each of cider and water until very soft. Sieve, then add 12 oz (350 g) of soft brown sugar for every pint (575 ml) of purée. Return to the pan and heat gently until thickened, then add ½ teaspoon each of ground cloves, ground cinnamon and ground nutmeg. When no excess moisture remains, pot and seal.

Apple drink

Save the skins from the apples, about 1½ lb (675 g), add the grated rind of 1 lemon, 1 tablespoon of sugar and 1 pint (575 ml) of boiling water. Infuse until cold, strain and serve as a refreshing drink.

To dry apples

Peel, core and cut into ¼-inch (0·5-cm) rings, and soak in salted water for 5 minutes. Dry in a cool oven (gas mark 1, 275°F, 140°C) for 6 to 8 hours, until leathery.

Apple pudding

To make a thrifty apple version of bread and butter pudding: peel, core and chop 1½ lb (675 g) of cooking apples. Butter a 2-lb (1-kg) pudding basin, line with thin slices of stale brown bread and butter, add half of the apples mixed with a little brown sugar, lemon rind and juice, then a layer of bread and butter, then the rest of the apple mixture, and finally top with more bread, buttered side down. Cover with greaseproof paper and steam for 1½ hours.

Barley wine

Cook 2 oz (50 g) of pearl barley in 3 pints (1·5 litres) of water for 3 hours. Strain (keep the barley for soup) and to the liquid add $\frac{1}{2}$ pint (275 ml) of red wine or port, 4 oz (125 g) of honey and 1 tablespoon of lemon juice. Serve warm.

To salt beans

Using 5 oz (150 g) of coarse salt for every 1 lb (450 g) of washed and dried French or runner beans, arrange in layers in an earthenware crock, starting and finishing with a layer of salt. Press down very tightly, cover, leave for a few days, then seal with a cork. Before cooking salted beans, soak in warm water for 2 hours.

Blackberry wine

Arrange alternate layers of washed blackberries and sugar in wide-mouthed jars, cover with muslin and leave for three weeks. Strain off the liquid and bottle it, adding a few raisins to each bottle. The wine will keep for up to a year.

Bramble jelly

Stew 1 lb (450 g) of washed blackberries with 6 fl oz (170 ml) of water in a covered pan for 20 minutes. Mash to squeeze out juice, then stir in 1 lb (450 g) of sugar and the juice of 1 lemon. When the sugar is entirely dissolved turn up heat and boil rapidly for 8 minutes, stirring occasionally. Strain through a nylon sieve into a warmed bowl, then transfer quickly (before the jelly sets) into warmed jars.

Quick pickled cabbage

Bring 2 pints (1 litre) of malt vinegar to the boil with 1 oz (25 g) of pickling spice, then remove from heat and leave for 4 hours. Strain the vinegar into a large bowl with 1½ lb (675 g) of cleaned and shredded red cabbage, add 1 tablespoon of coriander seeds, and transfer to clean preserving jars. Add some pieces of chilli pepper reserved from the pickling spices, seal and store for at least two months before eating.

Pickled cabbage will stay crisp indefinitely if you add a nut-sized lump of washing soda to the vinegar when you first boil it.

Chutneys

Home-made chutneys should be stored for at least three months, in a cool dark place, before eating.

Citrus fruits

Squeeze citrus fruits efficiently without a squeezer by cutting the fruit in half and driving a fork into the cut surface. Press down on the skin with one hand while turning the fork gently with the other.

To clarify jelly

If your fruit jelly is cloudy, add a few broken eggshells while it is simmering (and before you add the sugar). The sediment will cling to the shells, which can then be removed.

Coconuts

Pierce two of the eyes of a coconut to drain out the juice, then crack with a hammer. If the coconut resists, heat it in a moderate oven for twenty minutes, then cool.

Currants

Use a fork to strip blackcurrants or redcurrants from their stems.

Dried fruit

Save leftover tea and use it instead of water to soak and poach dried prunes, pears, peaches and apricots. There is a remarkable difference in flavour, at no extra cost.

Drying fruit

Wipe, halve and stone apricots or peaches and place cut side up on a rack, covered with muslin. Put in a very cool oven (gas mark $\frac{1}{4}$, 225°F, 110°C) with the door ajar and leave for two hours. Repeat every day for six days, then store in airtight containers.

Elderflower wine

Mash 6 elderflower heads with the juice and rind of 1 lemon. Add 1½ lb (675 g) of sugar, 2 tablespoons of white wine vinegar and 1 gallon (4 litres) of cold water. Cover and leave in a cool place for 24 hours, then strain into bottles, add screw-tops and leave for at least one week before drinking.

Floating fruit

When jam has reached setting point leave it to stand for fifteen minutes before potting it, so that the fruit will settle rather than rising to the top of each jar.

Freezer jam

If you have an abundance of soft fruit in the summer and want to make some instant, uncooked jam for freezing, crush 1¼ lb (550 g) of strawberries, raspberries, blackberries, or loganberries in a large bowl using a wooden spoon. Add 2 lb (900 g) of caster sugar and mix thoroughly, then leave to stand for 1 hour in a warm room, stirring occasionally.

Stir in 4 fl oz (125 ml) of commercial pectin, then 2 table-spoons of lemon juice. Stir for 2 minutes, then pour into clean, dry jars, cover and freeze.

Pickled gherkins

Scrub the gherkins with a stiff brush, then cover with boiling vinegar and leave for twenty-four hours. Drain, bring the vinegar back to the boil and return the gherkins to cook in it over a fierce heat until they become green again. Put the gherkins in glass jars, add a little salt, pepper, a few leaves of basil or marjoram or tarragon, and cover with the vinegar. When cold, seal and store in a cool place for at least two weeks.

Gooseberries

Add a head of elderflower to a pan of gooseberries to give them a grape-like flavour.

Home-made grape juice

Wash 1 lb (450 g) of grapes, place in a warm, sterilized 2-pint (1-litre) jar with ½ lb (225 g) of sugar, and fill up with boiling water. Seal the jar and leave upside down. Then store in a cool dark place.

Herb vinegar

Pick a handful of fresh herbs early in the morning, wash, dry and crush them and pour over them 1 pint (575 ml) of boiling cider or wine vinegar. Seal and leave for a fortnight, shaking vigorously once every day. Strain and seal with a cork.

Jam jars

Avoid subjecting jam jars to violent changes of temperature, or they may crack. Warm them before filling by placing upside down in a cold oven, then switching it on to gas mark ½, 250°F, 130°C. When they are filled with hot jam, do not put them on a cold surface, but on wood or a folded towel.

Jam kettles

A jam kettle should not be filled more than half full, otherwise the jam may boil over.

Never cook pickles, chutneys or any acid fruit or vegetables such as apples, rhubarb, blackcurrants or spinach in a copper, brass or aluminium pan: use one made of enamel or stainless steel.

Labels

Don't put labels on jars while they are still warm, or they will come unstuck.

Lemon curd

Heat together in a double boiler, or a basin standing in a pan of simmering water, 1 lb (450 g) of sugar, 4 oz (125 g) of butter, 4 beaten eggs, and the grated rind and juice of 4 lemons. Stir until sugar dissolves and heat, stirring occasionally, until the curd thickens. Strain into pots and cover.

Melon

Cut a slice off the bottom of each portion of melon before serving, so that it sits firmly on the plate.

Mould

If you seal jam while it is warm it is more likely to develop mould. Instead, seal it either when it is very hot, as soon as you have filled the jars, or when it has cooled right down.

A lemon-scented geranium leaf placed on top of each jar of jam before you seal it helps to prevent mould.

If you do find mould on top of jam, simply spoon it out: the rest is perfectly good to eat.

Quick pickled onions

Peel 1 lb (450 g) of pickling onions, half-fill a clean preserving jar with them, sprinkle with 1 dessertspoonful of pickling spice, then add more onions to fill the jar. Cover with ¾ pint (425 ml) of malt vinegar and seal with a plastic-coated screw-top. Store for at least eight weeks, and not more than four months, before eating.

Pickled onion jar

To get rid of the smell from an empty pickled onion jar, fill it with cold water, add a teaspoon of bicarbonate of soda, and leave to stand overnight.

Oranges

If you need to remove all of the pith from oranges for a decorative dessert, you will find it much easier if you let the oranges steep in boiling water for five minutes before peeling.

Orange marmalade

To make 6 lb (2·7 kg): squeeze 2 lb (1 kg) of Seville oranges and 1 lemon, add the juice and finely shredded peel to 4 pints (2·25 litres) of water in a preserving pan, and tie the pips and pith in a piece of muslin. Suspend this in the pan and simmer the fruit gently, uncovered, for 2 hours. Add 4 lb (1·8 kg) of warmed sugar and stir until dissolved, squeeze the muslin bag to extract all the jelly-like substance, then boil the marmalade rapidly for 10 minutes or until setting. Leave to settle for 20 minutes before potting.

Paper circles

Use waxed paper from breakfast cereals to make your own waxed paper circles to seal preserves. Always use waxed side down.

Pectin

To test the pectin content of cooked fruit, before potting, take 1 teaspoon of fruit juice from the pan, cool it and add 3 teaspoons of methylated spirit. Shake together, and if there is a high pectin content they will form a jelly.

Covering pickles

Always use plastic-coated screw-on lids to seal pickle and chutney jars. The vinegar in the pickles would corrode metal lids, and paper covers, which are not completely airtight, would allow the vinegar to evaporate.

Pineapple

Use a small biscuit cutter, potato peeler or apple corer to remove the hard core from slices of fresh pineapple.

Home-salted pork

Mix 8 oz (225 g) each of salt and sugar with 2 oz (50 g) of saltpetre, 1 oz (25 g) of juniper berries, 2 teaspoons each of peppercorns and crushed bay leaves and 1 teaspoon of dried thyme. Rub the mixture all over a piece of belly pork, then bury the meat in the remainder, cover with a weighted board and leave for at least five days.

Raspberry jam

Simmer 4 lb (2 kg) of hulled raspberries in their own juice for 20 minutes, or until soft. Add the same weight of sugar, stir until dissolved, then boil rapidly for about 10 minutes until setting point is reached. Pot and cover.

Quick redcurrant jelly

Heat 2 lb (1 kg) of redcurrants, stalks and all, in a preserving pan for 10 minutes, stirring to press out juices. Add 2 lb (1 kg) of warmed sugar, stir until dissolved, then boil rapidly for 8 minutes. Strain through a nylon sieve, then pot and seal.

Rhubarb chutney

Cook 2½ lb (1·25 kg) of chopped rhubarb, 8 oz (225 g) of finely chopped onion, 1 lb (450 g) of sugar, 1 level tablespoon each of ground ginger and curry powder, 1 teaspoon of salt and ⅜ pint (210 ml) of vinegar together slowly for 15 minutes. Add another ⅜ pint (210 ml) of vinegar and continue cooking until thick and jam-like. Pour into warmed jars, seal with plastic lids, and store for at least one month before eating.

Scum

Two tablespoons of vinegar added to the water you use for sterilizing jars will prevent scum forming on the contents.

Rub the inside of your jam kettle with butter before making jam to prevent sticking and prevent scum forming.

Or, stir a lump of butter into the jam when it is ready to set and this will disperse scum.

Setting

Remove the pan from the heat while you are testing for a set, otherwise you risk over-cooking the jam.

If jam will not set, add a tablespoon of lemon juice for every 1 lb (450 g) of fruit.

If after you have potted the jam you discover that it is not setting, stand the jars in a baking tin full of hot water and place in the oven at gas mark ½, 250°F, 130°C for a few minutes.

Sieves

It is best to use nylon sieves for puréeing fruit and tomatoes, as the acid in them might react with a metal sieve.

To sterilize jars

Wash and rinse thoroughly, then place in a cold oven, switch on at gas mark ½, 250°F, 130°C, and leave for ten minutes. The jars will now be sterile.

Stewing fruit

You will need less sugar to sweeten fruit if you add it after the fruit is cooked.

Straining jelly

When straining jelly through muslin, fix the cloth or bag to a large embroidery ring to hold it open.

Strawberry jam

To ensure that strawberries remain whole in jam, when you have hulled them place them in the preserving pan, cover with the sugar you are going to use for the jam and leave to stand overnight. This makes them firmer.

Do not wash strawberries before making them into jam, and do not use strawberries which have just been rained on. Excess moisture will prevent the jam setting. The boiling process in any case sterilizes the fruit.

Sugar

Heat the sugar for jam-making in a bowl in the oven while you are cooking the fruit, to speed up the dissolving process when you combine them.

Thermometers

Warm a thermometer gently in water before putting it into hot jam, or it may crack.

Famous Hints

The hints in this chapter come from well-known cookery writers who, as I had suspected, have some of the most ingenious ideas about saving time and money in the kitchen, and very kindly agreed to share them. They range from successful Yorkshire pudding to a quick hollandaise; how to keep parsley indefinitely to roasting new potatoes; non-weeping meringues to a substitute for wine. It's a fascinating collection: some real secrets of success!

Sonia Allison

'To remove the smell of fresh fish from hands, rub with dry mustard and then rinse off under warm water.'

Susan Campbell

'My favourite time-saving culinary tip is for making hollandaise sauce in about as many seconds as it takes to pour a cup of tea – but it's risky if you are an inexperienced cook. The method is quite simple: you beat the egg yolk(s) with a little lemon juice and water, using a small whisk, then heat the butter until it foams. Pour it, in a thin steady stream, on to the egg, whisking all the time. The hot butter cooks the egg just enough to thicken it to a proper consistency: if the butter isn't hot enough it doesn't work, and if it's too hot it curdles, so be a bit careful. Use exactly the same ingredients as if you were making a hollandaise in the normal way.' (i.e., 2 egg yolks, 2 tablespoons lemon juice, 1 tablespoon of water, 4 oz [125 g] of butter, salt and pepper.)

'I have another dodge: for removing the burnt black parts of over-cooked pastry shells, just chafe them with a sharp grater.'

'Also, I recommend skinning game birds, feathers and all, to save plucking them. If you are going to make a pie or casserole, you don't want the skins anyway, and it saves a great deal of time if you remove the skin and feathers together.'

Rose Elliot

'Replace half the cream in a quiche or fruit-based ice cream with low-fat soft white cheese (fromage blanc) for a lighter, healthier and less fattening version.'

'For a quick sauce to serve with plainly cooked foods add two tablespoons of chopped fresh herbs, a tablespoonful of single cream and salt and freshly ground black pepper to ¼ pint (150 ml) natural yoghurt.'

'When the oven is on you can melt chocolate quickly and easily by breaking the chocolate into pieces, putting them into a bowl and placing in a moderate oven for about ten minutes, until the chocolate is soft.'

'The flavour of hazel nuts is improved if you roast them before use. Spread the nuts on a dry baking sheet and bake in a moderate oven for about fifteen minutes, until the skins loosen and the nuts underneath are golden. Cool. The skins can be left on or rubbed off in a soft cloth.'

Theodora FitzGibbon

'To remove black skin from small thin fish fillets: heat a grill or a dry frying pan until very hot, then put the fillets under the grill skin side up, or in the pan skin side down, for 1 minute. Remove from heat and the skin will peel off easily. You can then continue cooking in whatever way you want.'

'Likewise for smoked haddock, put skin side down when poaching, then turn over after 2 minutes, slide off skin and continue cooking.'

Jane Grigson

'Wash your hands and utensils in *cold* water after dealing with any fish, particularly smoked fish: this gets rid of the smell.'

'Use kitchen paper for filtering things, if you run out of muslin.'

'Freeze stocks in ice cube trays.'

'Never waste shrimp and prawn or lobster and crab shells, but use to make a cheap good bisque.'

'If you don't have enough shells – or meatbones – all at once for making stock, store in the freezer until you do.'

'I combine chicken carcases and fish debris to make a splendid fish stock.'

'If a recipe demands fish stock when I haven't got any, I use chicken or light veal stock, with a splash of wine vinegar and wine.'

'If I have no wine for a stew, I use a tablespoon of wine vinegar plus two sugar lumps.'

'Dry orange peel and store to add to stews and fish sauces.'

'To freeze parsley, cram the sprigs into a plastic tub and jam on the lid. Don't add any water. This leaves you with a block from which you can grate what you require.'
   Or, mix fresh herbs with a minute amount of water and purée in a food processor or blender. Freeze in plastic egg cartons. This is very good for keeping things like fresh coriander if you do not have a regular supply.'

'Brush bread with water after baking, then return to the oven for 2 minutes. This gives a nice mild sheen, and is cheaper than using milk.'

'If you have small quantities of various flours – oatmeal and so on – mix them together to make bread. Almost any combination works, and makes good surprises. I often mix cornmeal and oatmeal, which works well.'

'Never blanch almonds before grinding them, just rinse if they seem dusty and dry.'

'If you have a solid fuel or oil-fired stove that is always on, bake meringues for 24 hours in the plate-warming oven.'

'Add a good pinch of cream of tartar to meringues and they seem to weep less.'

Elizabeth Kent

'For a change, try "roasting" new potatoes rather than boiling them. Take a large, heavy skillet or frying pan with a lid and melt 1–1½ oz (25–40 g) of butter in it. Scrub the new potatoes well and put an even layer of them in the pan.

Give a generous sprinkling of coarse sea salt, then cover the pan tightly. Cook over a very low heat for about 1 hour, shaking the pan from time to time. The potatoes should be beautifully browned, with a slightly nutty flavour.

Or, place the potatoes, well scrubbed, on a square of foil. Add a few knobs of butter with a good seasoning of sea salt and black pepper, then wrap tightly in the foil and bake in a moderately hot oven (gas mark 5, 375°F, 190°C) for 1 hour until just tender. Take out and leave for 5 minutes, then transfer the potatoes and juices to a serving dish.'

Prue Leith

'To clarify butter, melt it and strain it through fine muslin or a folded J-cloth – much easier than the usual method.'

'To avoid the need for basting roast chicken, etc., dip a piece of muslin or a pre-boiled J-cloth (you need to boil it to stop the colour running) in melted butter and lay it over the bird. The skin will brown through the cloth and the cloth will trap sufficient fat to provide continual basting.'

Delia Smith

Delia Smith has four rules to remember when making a quiche, 'to eliminate – for ever – the problem of the soggy pastry base.'

1. 'Use a metal container, not porcelain or glass.'
2. 'Stand the container on a baking sheet in the oven.'
3. 'Pre-bake the pastry case for 15 minutes.'
4. 'Then brush it with beaten egg (taken from the filling) and return the case to the oven for 5 minutes before adding the filling.'

She also has three tips for making Yorkshire puddings:
1. 'Use plain flour.'

2. 'Use a metal container.'
3. 'Pre-heat the oven.'

Michael Smith

'The most useful tip I can think of is my prolific use of biological washing powders: ideal for cleaning sticky hob pan rings, and all wooden spoons and spatulas get an overnight soak every now and then.'

'Tea towels, which are legion, are always in a pristine state when dumped overnight into a bucket of Ariel, and this treatment cleans pans better than anything I know of.'

Katie Stewart

'Rub the cut side of a lemon half round the inside of the mixing bowl before cracking in egg whites, and when you whisk them up you will get a much better volume – the acid stabilizes the foam. I always do this for meringue mixtures, especially those to go on top of hot puddings.'

Marika Hanbury Tenison

'Save all carrot peelings, celery trimmings, tomato and green pepper cores and seeds, mushroom peelings and onion skins to give stock flavour, goodness and colour.'

Weights and Measures

Approximate metric equivalents

Use these tables as a guide when converting recipes.

Weight

OUNCES	GRAMMES	OUNCES	GRAMMES
1	25	9	250
2	50	10	275
3	75	11	300
4	125	12	350
5	150	13	375
6	175	14	400
7	200	15	425
8	225	16	450

Liquid

PINTS	LITRES
$\frac{1}{4}$	150 ml
$\frac{1}{2}$	275 ml
$\frac{3}{4}$	425 ml
1	575 ml
$1\frac{1}{2}$	875 ml
2	1 litre

Oven temperatures

	ELECTRICITY		GAS
	F	C	
very cool	225	110	$\frac{1}{4}$
	250	130	$\frac{1}{2}$
cool	275	140	1
	300	150	2
moderate	325	170	3
	350	180	4
moderately hot	375	190	5
	400	200	6
hot	425	220	7
	450	230	8
very hot	475	240	9

Food portions

When shopping and cooking, allow the following amounts per person:

soup	$\frac{1}{2}$ pint (250 ml)
fish	4–6 oz (125–175 g)
meat without bone	6 oz (175 g)
meat with bone	8 oz (225 g)
green vegetables	4–6 oz (125–175 g)
potatoes	6–8 oz (175–225 g)
rice and pasta as	
accompaniment/starter	2 oz (50 g)
as main course	4 oz (125 g)

Index

Aligot, 88
Almonds, preparing, 148
Anchovies, de-salting, 70
Ants, deterring, 18
Aphids, deterring, 17, 18
Apple butter, 134
Apple drink, 134
Apple pudding, 134
Apples, baked, 118; drying, 134; growing in tubs, 15; mildew on, 17; peeling, 134
Artichokes, preparing and cooking, 96
Asparagus, deterring pests, 18; tinned, opening, 27
Avgolemono (Greek lemon sauce), 110
Avocado dip, 56
Avocado soup, 64
Avocados, storing, 22

BLT, 56
Baby foods, heating thriftily, 31
Bacon, over-salty, 73, 74; using rinds and trimmings, 74, 110
Bacon, beans and rice, 81
Baking, 124–32; blind, 130
Banana boats, 118
Banana nut cream, 119
Bananas, storing, 22
Barbecue grill, cleaning, 38
Barbecue sauce, 110
Barley wine, 135
Basil, growing, 12; used to deter pests, 18; storing, 23

Basins, identifying, 50; floury, cleaning, 42
Bean and pasta soup, 81
Beans, deterring pests, 13, 17, 18, 19; salting, 135; dried, cooking, 96; French, preparing and cooking, 96–7
Beer, leftover, 31
Beeswax polish, quick, 38–9
Beetroot, cooking, 97
Beurre manié, 111
Biological washing powders, uses, 150
Biscuit crumbs, 120
Biscuits, cutting out, 125
Blackberry wine, 135
Blackcurrant *brûlée*, 119
Blackfly, deterring, 18
Borage, 12
Bortsch, 65
Bouquet garni, home-made, 111
Brass, cleaning, 39; tarnishing, 39
Brassicas, deterring pests, 17, 18
Bread, soda, 107; wheatmeal, 108; yeastless, 108
Breadcrumbs, home-made, 103; substitute, 103
Breadmaking, 103, 148
Bread sauce, 111
Brie, chalky, 23
Brown sugar, hard, 125; substitutes, 50
Bubble and squeak, 88
Buckwheat pancakes, 119

Bulgur, 104
Burns, soothing, 51
Burnt stew, 51
Butchers, choosing, 69–70
Butter, hard, 125; rancid, 54;
　using thriftily, 31–2
Buttermilk, home-made, 32
Butterscotch sauce, 119

Cabbage, cooking, 97; quick
　pickled, 135–6
Cabbage moths, deterring, 18
Cacti, feeding, 13
Cakemaking, 125–9
Cake tins, 125
Cakes, icing, 126; serving, 127;
　storing, 127; fruit, flatter and
　richer, 126; all-in-one fruit, 126;
　party, 127; all-in-one sponge,
　127; Valentine's, 127
Caramel, 128
Caramel sauce, 120
Carrot fly, deterring, 13, 18
Carrot soup, 65
Carrots, maximizing flavour, 97;
　French-style, 97
Caterpillars, deterring, 16
Cauliflower, *au gratin*, 98; cooking
　leaves, 98; sautéed, 98;
　minimizing smell, 98
Celery, extra crisp, 98; used to deter
　pests, 18
Ceramic tiles, cleaning, 40
Chantilly cream, 128
Chapati, 104
Chapped hands, 51
Cheese, grating, 23; storing, 23
Cheesecake, instant, 120
Cheese soup, 65
Chicken, fried, 72; roast, 72;
　self-basting, 149
Chicken bricks, cleaning, 40
Chicken liver risotto, 81
Chips, perfect, 88
Chives, growing, 13; used to deter

pests, 18; substitute, 114
Chocolate, buying, 32; melting, 146;
　substitute, 51
Chocolate mousse, 120
Chrome, cleaning, 40
Chutney, home-made, storing, 136;
　rhubarb, 142
Cider, cooking with, 112
Cinnamon toast, 56
Citrus fruit, squeezing, 136
Cleaning, 37–48; products, 38, 40
Cobbler, 131
Coca Cola, used to remove stains,
　47
Cockroaches, deterring, 46
Coconuts, cracking, 136
Cod's roe, preparing, 71
Coffee filters, substitute, 51
Colcannon, 89
Compost heap, 13–14
Condensation, preventing, 41
Cookers, cleaning, 41, 43
Cook's feet, reviving, 51
Coriander, 14
Cornbread, 104
Corn-on-the-cob, preparing, 98
Corned beef, slicing, 27
Courgette flowers, preparing, 56
Courgette soup, 65
Crackling, carving, 77; crisper, 75
Cream, storing, 24; substitutes, 32,
　51, 52, 146; Chantilly, 128
Crisps, home-made, 56
Croque monsieur, 56
Crumble, 131
Crumpets, home-made, 57
Cucumber, preventing indigestion,
　98–9
Cucumber and yoghurt soup, 66
Cucumbers, deterring pests, 17, 19
Curd cheese, home-made, 32
Currants, preparing, 136
Curry, too hot, 53
Custard, egg, 120; uncurdling, 112
Cutlery, silver, cleaning, 44

Damp cupboard, 24
Dandelions, growing, 14
Decanters, cleaning and drying, 41
Dhal, 105
Dill, 14
Drains, frozen, 52
Duck, roasting, 73; Peking, 73
Dustbin raiders, deterring, 46
Dusters, impregnated, 42

Egg and lemon soup, 66
Egg whites, beating, 128–9, 150
Eggs, boiling, 57; poaching, 58;
    separating, 128; *en cocotte*, 57;
    Florentine, 82; framed, 57

Fabric softener, improvised, 47
Farmhouse supper, 89
Feathers, spin-drying, 47
Fennel, 14
Ferns, care of, 14–15
Fire, extinguishing, 52
Fish, 70–1; freezing, 24; grilling,
    71; removing smell, 145, 147;
    skinning, 147
Fish chowder, 66
Fish and potato soup, 82
Fish stock, home-made, 147
Flapjacks, 58
Flies, deterring, 46
Floors, cleaning, 42
Flowerholders, improvised, 15
Frankfurters, 82
French beans, 96
French toast, 58
French-style carrots, 97
Fried bread, crunchier, 58
Fried cheese sandwiches, 58
Frozen drains, 52
Fruit, 133–44; drying, 137; freezing,
    24; ripening, 24; sieving, 143;
    stewing, 143; dried, soaking, 137
Fruit fool, 120
Fruit trees, growing in tubs, 15

Frying pans, cast-iron, cleaning, 40
Frying problems, 53
Fuel, saving, 33

Game, skinning for pies, 146;
    storing, 24
Gammon steaks, preventing
    curling, 75
Garlic, cooking: 113; crushing, 113;
    in roasts, 75; growing: enemies,
    19; used to deter pests, 16, 18
Garlic bread, with herbs, 59
Gherkins, pickled, 138
Glass, washing, 42
Gooseberries, adding flavour, 138
Gougère, 131
Grape juice, home-made, 138
Graters, cleaning, 45; substitute, 42
Gravy, brown without browning,
    113
Grilling, fish, 71; meat, 75, 77, 78
Guacamole, 59

Ham, dried up, 52; over-salty, 75;
    boiled, juicier, 75
Hamburgers, perfect, 76
Hands, chapped, 51; softening, 53;
    stained, 53
Hasty pudding, 121
Hazelnuts, improving flavour, 146
Heather, preserving, 17
Herb soup, 66
Herbal tea, 12
Herbs, growing, 11, 15–16; used to
    deter pests, 18; storing, 148;
    dried, in cooking, 112
Herring, boning, 71
Hollandaise sauce, quick, 145
Home fries, 90
Horseradish, growing, 15; used to
    deter pests, 18
Horseradish sauce, 113
Houseplants, care in cold weather,
    13; feeding, 14

Ice cream, pudding, 121; sauces, 119, 120
Indigestion, curing, 53; preventing, 98, 100
Irons, cleaning, 42

Jam, freezer, 137; raspberry, 142; strawberry, 143
Jam jars, 138
Jam kettles, 139
Jam making, 135–44
Janssons temptation, 90
Jelly, clarifying, 136; straining, 143; bramble, 135; quick redcurrant, 142
Jelly cream, 121
Jerusalem artichoke soup, 67
Junket, 121

Kettles, preventing fur, 43
Kidneys, preparing, 76; in sherry sauce, 33
Kippers, jugged, 71; minimizing smell, 71

Labels, ensuring sticking, 139
Lamb, roast, serving, 76
Lasagne, 105
Latkes, 91
Leaking vase, 16
Leek and potato soup, 67
Leeks, cooking, 99; used to deter pests, 18
Leftovers, 31, 33, 35, 36, 73
Lemon curd, 139
Lemon flan, 122
Lemon soufflé omelette, 122
Lentil soup, 82
Lettuce, deterring pests from, 17; used to deter pests, 18; storing, 25; in salads, 99
Lettuce soup, 67
Linoleum, cleaning, 43
Liver, slicing, 77; tenderizing, 76
Lobsters, judging freshness, 71
Lovage, 16

Mace substitute, 113
Mange tout, cooking, 99
Marigolds, used in cooking, 16; used to deter pests, 19
Marmalade, orange, 140–1
Marrows, deterring pests, 19
Mayonnaise, made in blender, 114; storing, 114
Meat, 69–70, 73–8; beating, 74; browning, 75; carving, 75; grilling, 75; larding, 76; roasting, 77; storing, 25
Meatballs, 33
Melba toast, 59
Melons, deterring pests, 19; serving, 139; storing, 25
Meringues, 129, 148, 150
Mice, deterring, 46
Mildew, controlling, 17
Milk, used as anti-pest spray, 17; sour, uses, 35
Mince, stretching, 34
Mint, curbing, 17; used to deter pests, 18
Mint sauce, 114
Mouldy jam, 139–40
Mozzarella, storing, 25
Mushrooms, storing, 25
Muslin substitutes, 147, 149
Mustard, mixing, 114

Nasturtiums, growing and eating, 17
Nettles, 18
Nylon, whitening, 47

Oatcakes, 105
Olives, storing, 26
Omelette, *fines herbes*, 59; lemon soufflé, 122; sweet, 122
Onion and potato soup, 94
Onions, cooking: chopping, 100; minimizing smell, 100; quick pickled, 140; growing: enemies, 19; used to deter pests, 18

Orange cream, 123
Orange marmalade, 140–1
Orange peel, in stews, 148
Oranges, grilled, 122; removing pith, 140
Ovens, cleaning, 43
Oxtail stew, 34

PVC, cleaning, 43
Pan Haggerty, 91
Pancakes, lighter and quicker, 129; storing, 129; buckwheat, 119; potato, 92; seafood, 83
Parsley, cooking, 115; growing, 18; storing, 26, 148
Parsley butter, 115
Pasta, home-made, 105–6
Pastry, alternative, 130; burnt, 146; substitutes, 130–1; quick flaky, 130
Pastrymaking, 129–32, 149
Pâté, smoked mackerel, 61
Pea soup, 67
Peaches, ripening, 24
Peanut butter, home-made, 60
Pea pod soup, 68
Pears, growing in tubs, 15; ripening, 24
Peas, enemies, 19; deterring pests, 17; French-style, 100
Pectin, testing for, 141
Peking Duck, crisper, 73
Peppers, peeling, 100
Pests, garden, 13, 15, 16, 17, 18, 18–19; household, 46
Pet food dishes, improvised, 34
Pickled gherkins, 138
Pickled onions, 140
Pickles, sealing, 141
Picnic bottles, thrifty, 34
Pie funnel, substitute, 131
Pie plates, for freezing, 34
Pies, identifying, 26
Pillows, spin-drying, 47
Pineapple, coring, 141

Piperade, 60
Pizza, 83
Plastic bags, sealing, 26
Polenta, 106
Polyester, whitening, 48
Popcorn, home-made, 107
Poppadums, 60
Pork, carving, 77; cleaning, 77; salting, 141; with apple rings, 77
Porridge, authentic, 107
Potato: croquettes, 89; gnocchi, 89; pancakes, 92; salad, 92; scones, 93
Potato and onion soup, 94
Potatoes, cooking: 87–94; baked, 88; hashed brown, 90; mashed, 91; new, 91, 148–9; oven-fried, 91; parsleyed, 92; quick sauté, 92; Russian, 93; soufflé, 93; steamed, 94; growing: deterring pests, 18, 19
Potted beef, 61
Poultry, 72–3; drawing, 72; plucking, 72; roasting, 72; stuffing, 72
Puddings, 113–23; steaming, 132; apple, 134
Propagator, home-made, 19

Quiche, seafood, 84; unsoggy, 149

Radishes, deterring pests, 18
Raspberry jam, 142
Redcurrant jelly, 142
Refrigerator, care of, 22; cleaning, 44; smelly, 26
Rhubarb, used to deter pests, 18; chutney, 142
Rice, keeping hot, 107
Rice and peas, 83
Rissoles, 35
Roasts, 72–8
Rolls, yeastless, 108
Root rot, 13
Rosemary, used to deter pests, 18

Roses, propagating, 19
Rösti, 93

Saffron, maximizing flavour, 115
Sage, used to deter pests, 18
Salad, potato, 92; three-bean, 101; tuna and bean, 85
Salad servers, 100
Salad soup, 35
Salads, dressing, 99; garlic-flavoured, 99
Salt, quantities used, 115
Salty problems, 54, 70, 73–4, 75
Sandwiches, recycled, 35; thrifty, 32, 61; BLT, 56; *croque monsieur*, 56; fried cheese, 58
Saucepans, cleaning: aluminium, 38; burnt, 39; caramel, 40; cast-iron, 40; non-stick, 43; scrambled egg, 44
Sauces, lumpy, 54; smoother, 116; barbecue, 110; bread, 111; cheese, 112; quick cream and herb, 146; Greek lemon, 110; quick hollandaise, 145; horseradish, 113; mint, 114; tartare, 116; tomato, 116
Sausages, freezing, 26
Scones, lighter, 132
Scrambled eggs, stretching, 35
Scum on jam, 142
Seafood pancakes, 83
Seafood quiche, 84
Seasoning, 50, 72, 77, 112
Seedlings, protecting, 20; watering, 19
Seeds, roasting, 61; sowing, 13, 15–16, 19
Silk, laundering, 48
Silver, cleaning, 44
Sinks, cleaning, 44
Slugs, deterring, 16
Sock hanger, improvised, 48
Soups, enriching, 64; fatty, 52; freezing, 27; thickening, 64; avocado, 64; bean and pasta, 81; Bortsch, 65; carrot, 65; cheese, 65; courgette, 65; cucumber and yoghurt, 66; egg and lemon, 66; fish chowder, 66; fish and potato, 82; herb, 66; Jerusalem artichoke, 67; leek and potato, 67; lentil, 82; lettuce, 67; pea, 67; pea pod, 68; peanut, 68; potato and onion, 94; salad, 35; spinach, 85; split pea, 83; tomato, cold, 68
Sour cream, substitutes, 32, 52
Sour milk, uses, 35
Spaghetti, with butter and Parmesan, 80; carbonara, 84; with chicken livers, 84; with clams, 88; with mushrooms and peas, 85
Spinach, improving flavour, 101
Spinach soup, 85
Split pea soup, 83
Stainless steel, cleaning, 44
Stains, 45, 47
Sterilizing jars, 143
Stock, 147, 150; clarifying, 112; storing, 147; beef, 111, 112; fish, 147
Stock cubes, storing, 27
Storage, 21–9
Stovies, 94
Strawberries, enemies, 18; deterring pests, 19
Stuffing, 77; poultry, 72
Sugar, in jam making, 144; brown, hard, 125; substitutes, 50
Sweetbreads, preparing, 78; fried, 36
Sweet potato, growing, 20
Swiss roll, instant, 123
Syllabub, 123
Syrup, weighing, 36

Tablecloths, stained, 45
Tables, wooden, cleaning, 45

Tagetes minuta, used to deter pests, 19
Taramasalata, 61
Tarragon, maximizing flavour, 116
Tarts, decorating, 132
Thermometer, meat, 78; sugar, 144
Thyme, used to deter pests, 18
Tiles, ceramic, cleaning, 40
Tinned foods, 27
Toad-in-the-hole, 62
Toast, spreading, 62
Tomato ketchup, shaking the bottle, 36
Tomato soup, cold, 68
Tomatoes, deterring pests, 13, 17, 18, 19; ripening, 24
Tortillas, 108
Treacle, weighing, 36
Tuna and bean salad, 85
Tunafish cocktail, 86
Turkey, leftover, 73
Turnips, maximizing flavour, 101
Tzatziki, 62

U-trap, frozen, 52

Vanilla pods, recycling, 116
Vegetables, cooking thriftily, 33; over-salty, 54

Venetian blinds, cleaning, 45
Vinaigrette dressing, 101
Vinegar, herb, home-made, 138

Wallpaper, grease marks on, 45
Washing machines, overflowing, 47; using thriftily, 48
Watercress, storing, 27
Weevils, deterring, 16, 18
Welsh rarebit, 62
White sauce, filming, 113; curing lumps, 54; preventing lumps, 116; reheating, 115
Window boxes, watering, 20
Windows, cleaning, 45–6
Wine, leftover, 36; substitute in cooking, 148; barley, 135; blackberry, 135; elderflower, 137
Wireworms, deterring, 16
Wood, cleaning, 45, 46
Woollens, laundering, 48

Yeast, breadmaking without, 108; dried, 105
Yoghurt, stabilizing, 54
Yorkshire pudding, infallible, 149

Zabaglione, 123
Zinnias, used to deter pests, 19

Fontana Paperbacks
Non-fiction

Fontana is a leading paperback publisher of non-fiction.
Below are some recent titles.

The Round the World Air Guide *Katie Wood & George McDonald* £9.95
Europe by Train *Katie Wood & George McDonald* £4.95
Hitch-Hiker's Guide to Europe *Ken Walsh* £3.95
Eating Paris *Carl Gardner & Julie Sheppard* £2.95
Staying Vegetarian *Lynne Alexander* £3.95
Holiday Turkey *Katie Wood & George McDonald* £3.95
Holiday Yugoslavia *Katie Wood & George McDonald* £3.95
Holiday Portugal *Katie Wood & George McDonald* £3.95
Holiday Greece *Katie Wood & George McDonald* £5.95
Waugh on Wine *Auberon Waugh* £3.95
Arlott on Wine *John Arlott* £3.95
March or Die *Tony Geraghty* £3.95
Going For It *Victor Kiam* £2.95
Say It One Time For The Broken Hearted *Barney Hoskins* £4.95
Nice Guys Sleep Alone *Bruce Feirstein* £2.95
Impressions of My Life *Mike Yarwood* £2.95

You can buy Fontana paperbacks at your local bookshop or
newsagent. Or you can order them from Fontana Paperbacks,
Cash Sales Department, Box 29, Douglas, Isle of Man. Please
send a cheque, postal or money order (not currency) worth the
purchase price plus 22p per book for postage (maximum postage required is £3).

NAME (Block letters) _____

ADDRESS _____

_____

_____